Pilgrims and Peacemakers

Innumerable people have taken time to chat with me on my visits to the Holy Land. Many you will meet in the pages of this book. I cannot mention all by name—they are Palestinians and Jews, people of various religions (Christians, Jews and Muslims) or no religion. They have all given hospitality and shared their views and time—my grateful thanks to all of you.

Special thanks: to The Rt Revd Samir Kafity for his Preface and for hosting my visits to Jerusalem, and to John Tidy, the current Anglican Dean of St George's Cathedral, and Peter Crooks, the previous Dean who spent much time organizing my journeys; to Stephen Sizer who has been with me on several occasions and who came up with the idea for the theme of this book on a flight from Tel Aviv to Heathrow, February 1995; to Gill King who spent hours typing the whole book for me, twice—corrections and all—I am very grateful; to Beki Bateson, my PA at The Amos Trust, who kept the fax lines warm between Israel/Palestine and the Amos office.

GH

Garth Hewitt is World Affairs Advisor for the Guildford Diocese and Director of the Amos Trust—a justice and peace organization. Garth is also on the staff of St Saviour's, Guildford and is a Director of the Greenbelt Festival. He is a singer/songwriter and has over 20 albums and through his songs he seeks to tell stories of the forgotten and oppressed.

Contact address: St Saviour's Church, Woodbridge Road, Guildford, Surrey GU1 4QD, England. Fax: (44) 0 1483 453 593

Pilgrims & Peacemakers

A Journey Through Lent Towards Jerusalem

Garth Hewitt

The Bible Reading Fellowship
OPENING THE BIBLE

Published by
The Bible Reading Fellowship
Peter's Way, Sandy Lane West
Oxford OX4 5HG
ISBN 0 7459 3252 5
Albatross Books Pty Ltd
PO Box 320, Sutherland
NSW 2232, Australia
ISBN 0 7324 0946 2

First edition 1995
10 9 8 7 6 5 4 3 2 1 0

Acknowledgments
Unless otherwise stated, scripture is taken
from the New Revised Standard Version of the
Bible (NRSV) copyright © 1989 by the
Division of Christian Education of the National
Council of the Churches of Christ in the USA.

Song lyrics by Garth Hewitt © copyright
Word Music (UK) except 'We need your
mother love O God' © Chain of Love
Music.

A catalogue record for this book is
available from the British Library

Printed and bound in Great Britain by
Biddles Ltd, Guildford and King's Lynn

Contents

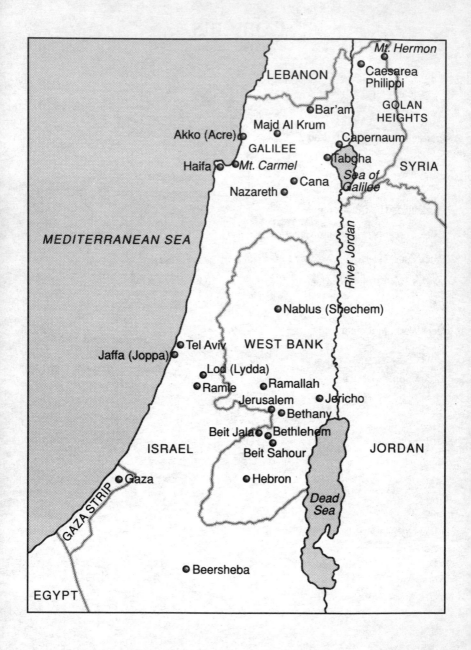

Preface
by Bishop Samir Kafity
Anglican Bishop in Jerusalem

Jerusalem has always been a place of pilgrimage. In every age and generation pilgrims without number have streamed through her gates seeking the inspiration and favour of the holy places. Within, the city walls embrace the faithful and the curious of every race, culture and creed. Without, they stand strong to protect and defend her sanctity: born of the divine presence, revealed in the drama of our salvation, made valid by the prayer and devotion of the tide of humanity that pours through her portals. An object of piety and curiosity, a focus of conflict and division, a symbol of peace and a glimpse of our ultimate destiny. All this and so much more is the holy city—Jerusalem.

Even though you may have never stood within her gates or have no desire to do so, the fascination and attraction of Jerusalem is undeniable. No other city in the world may boast the hill of Calvary. No other city hosts an Empty Tomb. From Jerusalem the Good News was first proclaimed. A constant prey to human pride and ambition, no other city may claim to be so great a prize, political and religious. Here the Church was born. Here Arab Christians, present since the day of Pentecost, have maintained a faithful witness in times of stability and turmoil.

As you journey to Jerusalem through these pages in heart and mind, in imagination and intent, be encouraged by the presence and the prayers of *the living stones* in this city and the land of Palestine. For *the living stones* are your brothers and sisters in Christ—Arab Christians like myself—who share this Lenten journey with a lively faith in the knowledge of the resurrection and in the hope of healing and wholeness, reconciliation and peace, justice and abundance of life. Such is the promise released from the Tomb at the dawning of the day. A promise which fills with hope and anticipation the desire for dignity and freedom, the yearning for justice and peace, the cry for release from hunger and pain.

From wherever you begin your journey the end is Jerusalem, the Mother City of our faith. Born into a Christian home, my journey began in Haifa. Together with my family I quickly became a refugee. The loss of dignity and freedom, the deprivations of injustice and oppression, and the aspirations of my people for justice and peace are a part of my inheritance. My story informs my faith and my faith informs my search for the new Jerusalem. My story is the story of generations of Palestinian Christians. It is the story of countless peoples in our world past and present. It is your story and mine as we engage in the journey of peace. Garth Hewitt invites us to share in the journey through the eyes of some of these fellow pilgrims and peacemakers. He invites us to walk in the company of Jesus who is the Way, the Truth and the Life. May our Lenten pilgrimage keep us ever faithful in the Way, lead us to a deeper understanding of his Truth, bring us to the Empty Tomb and fulness of Life.

Samir Hanna Kafity
Anglican Bishop in Jerusalem
Jerusalem, August 1995

Introduction

As we read the Gospels we find that there is a sense of Jesus 'setting his face towards Jerusalem'. Almost like a magnet it starts to draw him and the tempo begins to pick up as we journey relentlessly towards Holy Week. It is a journey that for us will go from the wilderness and its temptations, on a detour to Bethlehem and down to Egypt, then it will lead us through Galilee at a more relaxed pace, as Jesus teaches and heals, and then through the Jordan Valley to Jericho, and up towards Jerusalem. It is a journey towards crucifixion—it is a journey towards resurrection. As we follow Jesus on this journey, we can't help being aware that we are journeying through one of the most crucified parts of the world, and our prayer is that this too will be a journey towards resurrection—a journey towards peace. As we join Jesus as pilgrims on this journey, we shall be meeting some present-day local Christians and peacemakers *en route* and seeing what the good news of Jesus means to them. Let it be a journey of discovery, in which eyes are opened, as we learn more about following Jesus and more about one of the 'open wounds' of conflict of our world.

In 1996 Jerusalem is due to be on the agenda of the Palestinian–Israeli peace talks and, because of this, the Israeli government is making it the year of the 3,000th anniversary of King David conquering this Jebusite city and making it the centre of Judaism. The chronological basis for this may be shaky, and the motives may be political, but there is a very important lesson to be learnt from David's attitude. Karen Armstrong, talking about Jerusalem (at 'The Current Status of Jerusalem and the Future of the Peace Process' conference, 15–16 June 1995 in London) pointed out that David did not expel the Jebusites—he had no massacres like Joshua. Indeed, he expropriated the cult of the Jebusites on Mount Zion and grafted on to it the cult of the exodus, and the first priest of Yahweh in Jerusalem was a Jebusite—Zadok. David's tolerance in not expelling the Jebusites may give an example of a way forward in the peace talks for Jerusalem. Let this be a city for both Jew and Palestinian. For Jerusalem—Yerushalayim in Hebrew, and Al-Quds al-Sharif in Arabic—is seen as capital to two communities and as holy to three religions.

The city of peace has been a city of conflict—armies have attacked Jerusalem nearly forty times. Religion has often played a sordid part. In 1099 the crusaders arrived and for two days killed Muslims and Jews until the blood came up to the knees of their horses, and there were piles of bodies. The record is not good. Jesus wept over Jerusalem saying, 'If only you knew what made for peace.' We should also weep at the folly of humanity with its brutality, its war, its desire to exclude the other. Could this be the time when the city of peace could become just that, and welcome all? Pray for the peace of Jerusalem.

I came across some words from the Talmud (a commentary on the Jewish scriptures), which said this:

> *Ten measures of beauty God gave to the world,*
> *Nine to Jerusalem, one to the remainder.*
> *Ten measures of sorrow God gave to the world,*
> *Nine to Jerusalem and one to the remainder.*

Strange words, yet strangely true. This beautiful and fascinating city is so attractive, and yet here you feel the pain of history and you see the wounds of the present day. I turned these words into a song, with the refrain from Psalm 122:6 of praying for the peace of Jerusalem, and you might like to use it as a prayer for both Palestinian and Jewish communities, that there may be justice and peace for all, and that the wounds and bitterness of history may be healed.

> *Ten measures of beauty God gave to the world,*
> *Nine to Jerusalem, one to the rest;*
> *Ten measures of sorrow God gave to the world,*
> *Nine to Jerusalem, one to the rest.*

> *So pray for the peace, pray for the peace,*
> *Pray for the peace of Jerusalem.*

> *You can greet your friends with the word 'Shalom'*
> *Or you can greet them with 'Salaam'—*
> *But peace itself will never come*
> *Till there's justice for everyone.*
> *And there can be no peace for the Jew*
> *Till there's peace for the Palestinian, too;*
> *There can be no peace for the Jew*
> *Till there's peace for the Palestinian, too.*

> *So pray for the peace, pray for the peace,*

Pray for the peace of Jerusalem.

May the justice of God fall down like fire,
And bring a home for the Palestinian;
May the mercy of God fall down like rain,
And protect the Jewish people.
And may the beautiful eyes of a holy God
Who weeps for all His children
Bring the healing hope for His wounded ones—
For the Jew and the Palestinian.

So pray for the peace, pray for the peace,
Pray for the peace of Jerusalem.

Garth Hewitt

And pray for our own peace. As we make this journey, we will discover that the road to personal peace and satisfaction does not lie in putting ourselves first; it doesn't lie in ignoring the conflicts and the pain of our world; it doesn't lie in keeping quiet about issues of justice. It is those who hunger and thirst for justice who will find satisfaction; it is those who lose their life who gain it, those who give their lives for others and who refuse to allow bigotry, prejudice and selfishness to dominate. Following Jesus is not just a geographical exercise, it is a way of life. It is an attitude of mind and heart, it is taking up a cross, it is being a servant. But this road of self-denial and humility leads to satisfaction, joy and resurrection. It is the road of hope. The road certainly goes through the wilderness, through the events of Holy Week and Good Friday, but it leads to Easter Sunday.

Journey Through the Wilderness

We start our journey with Jesus heading for the desert. Our journey will end in Jerusalem and we begin not far away—just down the road towards Jericho. It is a windy old road which leads from Jerusalem to Jericho through a desert area. Everywhere has its traditional sites in the Holy Land—normally at least two for each event! If there is a traditional site for the temptations of Jesus then it is the Mount of Temptations, which is up from Jericho on the old road, west of Jericho and east of Jerusalem. The trip from Jerusalem to Jericho is spectacular. It starts at 800 metres above sea level and then the road plunges down through some of the most dramatic desert landscape to Jericho—the lowest city on earth at 250 metres below sea level. It is a winding, twisting road that goes through the limestone hills of the Judean desert, with small Bedouin camps on either side of the road. On this road you will find the Inn of the Good Samaritan, which is curious since Jesus simply used this setting for his parable of the Good Samaritan. It would seem likely, though, that there must have been some sort of traveller's rest here for thousands of years, especially bearing in mind that Jericho itself is the oldest known inhabited place on earth. Travellers to Jerusalem coming up from the Jordan valley would have gained their first view of the Mount of Olives and Mount Scopus from here. Standing overlooking the area known as Wadi Kelt there is a view of St George's monastery which seems to cling to the ravine edge on the other side of the valley. The first monastery was founded here in AD480 by John of Thebes, who for a time became Bishop of Caesarea, though much of the present building dates from crusader times and was restored by the Greek Orthodox Church towards the end of the ninteenth century.

But it's here, on this spot, that I look around and think about the temptations of Jesus. And if somewhere on this road we can think of Jesus facing his temptations after his baptism in the River Jordan, then it is also up this road that he comes as he 'sets his face towards Jerusalem'. Having been in Jericho, and having transformed the life of Zacchaeus, he will head up this dangerous road facing a different temptation—perhaps the temptation to have the cup of suffering taken away from him—the temptation he will face in the Garden of Gethsemane. Towards the end of Lent, we will follow Jesus again up this road, then see him pause at Bethany before heading across the Kidron Valley and into Jerusalem.

Ash Wednesday
No easy road

LUKE 4:1-4

Jesus, full of the Holy Spirit, returned from the Jordan and was led by the Spirit in the wilderness, where for forty days he was tempted by the devil. He ate nothing at all during those days, and when they were over, he was famished. The devil said to him, 'If you are the Son of God, command this stone to become a loaf of bread.' Jesus answered him, 'It is written, "One does not live by bread alone."'

There's something strangely beautiful about the desert, but also something that seems to put our humanity into perspective—something that seems to put ourselves into perspective. The desert is a place of stillness, indeed a place of silence where we come face to face with ourselves. Usually when we experience 'wilderness times', we look on these as negative—but they are often the place where we face up to ourselves with more honesty and they are the times that help us towards maturity, so we no longer stay as children in our faith but start to mature to adulthood. This is an important aspect of our lifetime pilgrimage for us to understand.

In Mark's Gospel the temptations only have two verses, but Matthew and Luke expand them and use the event as an opportunity for teaching. All of Jesus' replies to the devil come from chapters 6 to 8 in Deuteronomy and, in a way, the temptations are all about sinning against the great commandment to love God 'with all your heart, and with all your soul, and with all your might' (Deuteronomy 6:5).

There's a great humanity about the first temptation. Jesus was hungry, he was exhausted and alone and he was tempted to use power for his own selfish needs. It was a temptation to self-indulgence, to greed, a temptation to the easy life. And this is a daily temptation for us, to take the easy way out, not to discipline ourselves in areas of greed, materialism or even sensuality. And Jesus quotes from the passage in Deuteronomy which is focused on why God led his people through the wilderness, 'in order to humble you, testing you to know what was in your heart, whether or not you would keep his commandments. He humbled you by letting you hunger... in order to make you understand, that one does not live by bread alone, but by every word that comes from the mouth of the Lord.' Matthew includes this last sentence in his story of the temptation. And then in Deuteronomy, the passage that would have been very familiar to Jesus goes on to say that their clothes didn't wear out and their feet didn't swell during those forty years of wandering and God was disciplining them as a parent disciplines a child. Jesus is accepting that he needs the discipline of this time in the wilderness, not some easy way out. In the spirituality with which we are currently familiar, too often we look for an instant solution—'health and wealth' and we want it now. We want God to speak to us 'now', to guide us 'now', to heal us 'now'. These are particularly modern temptations. We want well-being and and materialism, and Jesus is saying to us, no—have patience, walk in the wilderness and discover how to rely on God. Simplify your lifestyle, reject the easy answers and the wilderness journey will start to teach you something about trust of God and how to love him with your heart, your soul and your mind.

The devil's temptation is subtle, 'If you are the Son of God...' go on prove yourself, otherwise how can we believe? Give us a sign, a wonder, a spectacle to prove yourself. Later on in Matthew we will hear this subtle temptation again, 'If you are the Son of God come down from the cross.' If... then we will believe. But it is a temptation again to take the easy road—let's have resurrection without crucifixion. But Jesus is teaching a deep truth—life isn't like that. People want easy roads to peace—don't mention the problems, gloss over them, keep silent, don't rock the boat. But this doesn't bring peace, it simply preserves the status quo. The two-edged sword of the gospel wounds before it can heal—but that wounding is also necessary.

Maybe you are faced today with an issue you would rather duck or skirt around. Don't take the easy road that appears to go around the conflict, go through even if it's costly and hard. Jesus said, 'Your will be done.' This should be our prayer, even if it doesn't give us the easy road we wanted—in the end it will be the road that satisfies more deeply.

Thought

How are you tempted to 'turn stones into bread'—to take the easy route? Could it be over-indulgence, security, sexual fantasies, or a desire to dominate others? Could it be some issue you know you should face—but you are avoiding? Try to isolate the temptation that is challenging you and then imagine using the words of Jesus to reject it.

The temptation to power

LUKE 4:5-8

Then the devil led him up and showed him in an instant all the kingdoms of the world. And the devil said to him, 'To you I will give their glory and all this authority; for it has been given over to me, and I give it to anyone I please. If you, then, will worship me, it will all be yours.' Jesus answered him, 'It is written, "Worship the Lord your God, and serve only him."'

This is the temptation for Jesus to go for power and wealth and to prefer this to the love of God. 'Glory' is the biblical word that symbolizes outward splendour or wealth. The term 'Son of God', which is used throughout this passage, makes Jesus a representative of Israel and these temptations of Jesus have a universal significance. Because Jesus stands for Israel he is the beginning of the new people of God, the founder of a new humanity. The basic temptation is not to love God in the way that should be the pattern of this new community. Each temptation reflects an aspect of this.

It is also the temptation to manipulate others. As a husband or a wife we can want to mould our partner and make the major decisions. At work we can try and manipulate people for our gain. People can play these games just as much in church and it's only as we resist the temptation to manipulate others that we allow them their dignity as human beings and that we show our full love of God and of our neighbour. The temptation is to love the wrong things. In other words, if Jesus worshipped the power of dominating these kingdoms he would be worshipping a false god because the true God will not dominate. From this God we learn that the way to live is to serve others.

The deal the devil was offering was power for idolatry. If you worship me—you can have it. Worship of weapons is idolatry. It certainly brings power but, in the end, a power that consumes. It is worship of the god of war. Recently I have been aware of the need for churches to lead the way in the rejection of weapons. I've been particularly conscious of this on visits to the United States and to South Africa, where I have seen the awful destructive effect of guns on their societies. I was reminded of a church in Mozambique during the civil war a few years ago where Bishop Dinis Singulane even encouraged children to bring in their toy guns to be destroyed because he wanted the romanticism of violence to be stopped. There is what Walter Wink calls 'the myth of redemptive violence'—but violence is not redemptive, it is destructive and it always destroys communities because it separates people. Without weapons we must learn to reach out our hands to each other. In our communities, where there is rising violence, we must teach our children another way. It is vitally important because redemptive violence is worshipped almost ceaselessly in Hollywood films. In the UK, where a large percentage of the workforce is now involved in making weapons, we need to call our country back to worship of God and not worship of an idol.

Worship of money is idolatry—it brings power but, again, it consumes. Our worship of money and the free market with no regulation has left Britain in a perilous situation. As Will Hutton, in his book, *The State We're In* says, 'Ungoverned British capitalism's lethal demand for some of the highest financial returns in the world has encouraged firms relentlessly to exploit their new freedom to hire and fire. As a result there is a mounting and quite proper sense of crisis… about the character and availability of work and its implications for every aspect of society—from the care of our children to the growing dereliction of our cities… Insecurity, low wages and wasted talent are widespread, and the problem touches professions and occupations once thought inviolable.' He goes on to point out the impact and the 'destructive consequences on human relations of an exclusive emphasis on the primacy of market forces'. There has been an idolatry that is consuming us. Jesus is rejecting idolatry: worship of the true God gives us the principles to build proper community. The deal the devil offers does give power—but it is destructive and, in the end, consuming. The first commandment says, 'You shall have no other gods before me.' Put God first. This is the rejection of selfishness. It's losing your life… so you can gain it.

Thought

What other idols do we worship, apart from war and wealth—prestige, security, fashion, family?

Prayer

Lord Jesus, you strengthen us when we are tempted. You spent forty days and nights suffering temptation in the wilderness and discerning which route reflected the love of God and which route was the cheap and easy option. Give us discernment, surrounded as we are by temptations, to see clearly, and your strength to help us overcome, so we can walk the way of love of God with heart, soul and mind. Amen.

Temptation to play 'Superman'

LUKE 4:9–13

Then the devil took him to Jerusalem, and placed him on the pinnacle of the temple, saying to him, 'If you are the Son of God, throw yourself down from here, for it is written, "He will command his angels concerning you, to protect you," and "on their hands they will bear you up, so that you will not dash your foot against a stone."' Jesus answered him, 'It is said, "Do not put the Lord your God to the test."' When the devil had finished every test, he departed from him until an opportune time.

We long for a 'Superman' figure and if only Jesus would show that he is a 'Superman', then the crowds would welcome him... but it's not the way of God. He doesn't court publicity. Isn't it strange that Jesus came before satellite television and mass media? Just imagine, he could have done the jumping down from the temple in front of the whole world live on CNN and we would have to believe! But it is not the way of God to manipulate us or to force us. Jesus came to a stable. He went and lived in a small town which was considered as somewhere insignificant at a time when there was none of the instant media access that we now have. But this, in its turn, says something about the ways of God.

This temptation reminds us not to court human praise, not to flaunt charismatic personalities, not to wield spiritual power in order to manipulate, not to test the Lord by doing stupid things. Sometimes Christians seem almost to worship the irrational, as if that must somehow be more 'spiritual'. This, too, can be a temptation—it can be a lack of trust. Jesus knew it was not the route of his death to jump from the temple. It would have shown a lack of trust in God's way and, therefore, a lack of love of God. We, too, should not try to manipulate God.

Note the devil quotes the Jewish scriptures to Jesus and we, too, can manipulate the scriptures to distort them or to make them say whatever we want. Be wary of taking verses out of context or letting too much hinge on one verse. Check that verse against others to see the wider context of the Bible. Also be wary of the 'horoscope' approach to the Bible, where we take one verse out of context and say God has spoken to us through this verse. It is not that this could not happen, but that we need to test it and make sure we are not simply making the Bible say something we want to hear.

Helmut Thielicke, in his book, *Between God and Satan*, says about this temptation that what the devil says is, to all appearances, very pious. It is misleading not only because it uses a 'religious phrase and the right and wrong use of the fact of God,' but also 'because it quotes the Bible and "Takes God at His word." That is the most dangerous mask possessed by the devil: the mask of God. It is more horrifying than the garment of light. Luther knew something about it. He was dreadfully afraid of it. He saw himself, as it were, encircled by God. He had to flee from God (from this masked demon) to God. This flight is one of the ultimate secrets of his faith. We must have stood in the desert beside Jesus Christ to be aware of it… Yes; the word of God, piety, worship, religion, miracles and signs are the mightiest signs of the wicked foe.' So the devil departs 'until an opportune time'. Thielicke warned of a 'God of power' who supersedes the God of the Bible. He was writing in 1939 in Germany and clearly he saw the danger of Nazism. A god of power was worshipped at the expense of the true God of the Bible, with all the horror that then emanated from this. Sadly, too many Christians went along with this god of power because they could not see the God of the Bible, and Thielicke wrote his book to encourage them to stand against temptation but, for the majority, the false god was too strong.

So, after testing Jesus, the devil departs 'until an opportune time'. This is a reminder that temptations are always with us, temptations to take the easy route, temptations to try and be the superhero and provide instant success, temptations to depart from the way of Jesus, temptations to the easy life or to the quiet life, which are idolatries because they put 'me' first instead of God. And what is offered instead by Jesus? A hard road, 'Enter through the narrow gate; for the gate is wide and the road is easy that leads to destruction, and there are many who take it. But the gate is narrow and the road is hard that leads to life, and there are few who find it.'

Prayer

Lord, your hard way was the way of the servant. Your power is not to dominate but to open people up to their full potential. Thank you for the hope this offers. May we be servants like you. Amen.

Who is my neighbour?

LUKE 10:29–37

'And who is my neighbour?' Jesus replied, 'A man was going down from Jerusalem to Jericho, and fell into the hands of robbers, who stripped him, beat him, and went away, leaving him half dead. Now by chance a priest was going down that road; and when he saw him, he passed by on the other side. So likewise a Levite, when he came to the place and saw him, passed by on the other side. But a Samaritan while travelling came near him; and when he saw him, he was moved with pity. He went to him and bandaged his wounds, having poured oil and wine on them. Then he put him on his own animal, brought him to an inn, and took care of him. The next day he took out two denarii, gave them to the innkeeper, and said, "Take care of him; and when I come back, I will repay you whatever more you spend." Which of these three, do you think, was a neighbour to the man who fell into the hands of the robbers?' He said, 'The one who showed him mercy.' Jesus said to him, 'Go and do likewise.'

Jesus places this parable on the road from Jerusalem to Jericho. Perhaps he was even travelling somewhere around this area on one of his journeys to Jerusalem. Whatever the circumstances, it was an ideal setting for this particular story. It was then—and, indeed, has been up until very recently—an extremely dangerous road.

It's sometimes hard for us to grasp the impact of this story because we are so familiar with it. It's a story that breaks down the barriers of religion and race and, therefore, has an extreme poignancy in the current situation in the Holy Land. Recently *Time* magazine printed an article about Bassam Kafisha, a Palestinian from Hebron, who discovered two Jewish settlers bleeding in an adjacent field to where he was working. They were Jewish settlers from the nearby Kiryat Arba and they had been attacked by a Palestinian assailant. Bassam did not hesitate to help these men, but after forty-five minutes no ambulance had arrived, so he lifted them into his own car and, driving towards a hospital in Hebron, he flagged down an Israeli military vehicle. The parallel is strikingly similar, and when he was asked why he had done it, he pointed out, 'At such a time you forget about politics, and you see these men as heads of families, as sons, as relatives' (Lisa Beyer, 'Dispatches', from *Time* magazine, 23 January 1995). For a Jew this would be comparable to the story of the Good Samaritan because a Palestinian would be of another religion—Muslim or Christian—and of another race and they too are a despised people, just as the Samaritans were.

It was the upholders of tradition and division who passed by on the other side—and Jesus is telling this story to bring out one theme—that of being a neighbour—and the way it breaks down barriers and the way it runs risks that can be costly. Sydney Carter's familiar song hits the nail on the head, 'When I needed a neighbour, were you there, were you there?... And the creed and the colour and the name won't matter, were you there?' To be a neighbour we must do loving acts that cross divisions. Pastor Niemoller, who was one of the leaders of the 'Confessing Church' in Germany during the Second World War, said these now familiar words, 'When they came for the communist I didn't speak up because I wasn't a communist. When they came for the Jew I didn't speak up because I wasn't a Jew. When they came for the trade unionist I didn't speak up because I wasn't a trade unionist. When they came for the Catholic I didn't speak up because I wasn't a Catholic. When they came for me there was no one left to speak up.'

This parable is really at the heart of the gospel, because Jesus has just had a discussion with a lawyer, who asks him, 'What must I do to inherit eternal life?' Jesus asks him what's written in the Law, and he responds by quoting, 'You shall love the Lord your God with all your heart, and with all your soul, and with all your strength, and with all your mind'; and then he adds, 'And your neighbour as yourself.' And Jesus points out that if you do this, you will live. It's then that the lawyers asks, 'Who is my neighbour?' He wants clarification and at the end of the parable when Jesus has then asked him which of the people was a neighbour, he responds, 'The one who showed him mercy.' Jesus cross questions this lawyer and uses him to give the right answers. Then he adds, 'Go and do likewise.'

Thought

Think of those with whom you have differences—people of a different religion, a different race, a different viewpoint. Are there certain people or types of people that you really can't stand? Put their name into the story in the place of the Samaritan. See what it does for the story and to your viewpoint... then 'go and do likewise'.

Sundays In Lent:
Places Jesus Didn't Go!

Lent consists of forty days, though if you count up all the days between Ash Wednesday and Easter you will discover there are forty-seven. This is because, technically, Sundays are not in Lent. Consequently, we will take Sunday as a day off on our journey and take little detours within the Holy Land. My theme is 'places Jesus didn't go'—as far as we know! Places that you may well visit on a pilgrimage to the Holy Land or places that are mentioned in the Bible, but not in conjunction with Jesus. And we hope this will give us an insight into some different parts of Israel/Palestine and the chance to meet further some of the local Christians and peacemakers.

The first Sunday we meet Winnie Tarazi from Gaza and then hear about a journey of peace to Gaza by a Jewish rabbi.

First Sunday
The road to Gaza

ACTS 8:26–35

Then an angel of the Lord said to Philip, 'Get up and go toward the south to the road that goes down from Jerusalem to Gaza.'... So he got up and went. Now there was an Ethiopian eunuch... He had come to Jerusalem to worship and was returning home; seated in his chariot, he was reading the prophet Isaiah. Then the Spirit said to Philip, 'Go over to this chariot and join it.' So Philip ran up to it and heard him reading the prophet Isaiah. He asked, 'Do you understand what you are reading?' He replied, 'How can I, unless someone guides me?'... Then Philip began to speak, and starting with this scripture, he proclaimed to him the good news about Jesus.

So today we find ourselves on the road heading from Jerusalem down to Gaza. And no doubt the Ethiopian eunuch we meet is going to head through Gaza into Egypt before going down to Ethiopia. For Luke, the writer of Acts, this is very significant because it is the gospel going to Africa. And, of course, Ethiopia has one of the most ancient churches that has maintained its witness through the centuries. It is interesting to see that the Ethiopian had gone to Jerusalem to worship, so he may have been a fully fledged proselyte or, at the very least, a Gentile God-fearer. The Ethiopian is reading a passage from Isaiah 53, one of the passages about the suffering servant, and we shall see this is regular Luke territory. He has Jesus quoting from Isaiah in the synagogue at Nazareth and there are similarities with the Emmaus road walk of Jesus as Philip, starting with this scripture, begins to unpack the good news about Jesus just as Jesus had done on that Emmaus walk. Jesus is recognized in Emmaus in the breaking of bread, whereas here it leads to another sacrament. The Ethiopian asks, 'Can I be baptized?'

We will head on, so to speak, down this road and into Gaza. Gaza is a symbolic place because it is on the crossroads between Africa and Asia. Consequently it has meant that, in history, it has been a troubled place and has been fought over, invaded and occupied. After the U.N. partition plan, thousands of Palestinians who had been expelled from villages along the coastal plain sought refuge in Gaza and almost overnight the population trebled. At this time it was administered by the Egyptians. The Israelis occupied Gaza for four months during the Suez crisis, but Gaza was overrun again during the Six Day War of 1967. Gaza is the most crowded piece of land on earth and it was here that the Intifada (literally, the 'shaking off') started. The Intifada was the uprising that started in 1987 which focused the world's attention on the plight of the Palestinians.

Gaza is predominantly a Muslim area, though there has been a regular Christian witness. Whenever I am there, I visit the Al Ahli Hospital, which is a Christian hospital originally set up by the Church Missionary Society and now administered by the Anglican Diocese of Jerusalem. Now that most of Gaza has been handed over to Palestinian rule, there is a new feeling abroad. Pray that the uncertain footsteps that have started on the pathway to peace may become more certain and that these people, who have been herded together for forty years in this crowded piece of land, may find a way forward to dignity. Pray for the Christians of Gaza today and the churches meeting in Gaza. There is a Baptist church, a very small Anglican community, Holy Family Latin Catholic Church, and St Perferious Greek Orthodox Church.

Winnie Tarazi from Gaza is a teacher for the women's secretarial course at the Near East Council of Churches. I told her about the subject of this book, and she responded: 'The subject *Pilgrims and Peacemakers: A Journey Towards Jerusalem* is a topic we always contemplate. Being a Palestinian and born in Jerusalem, who spent her early childhood and her years of high school there, Jerusalem to me is so close to my heart and I feel with nostalgia towards that city which is not like any other city for its holiness.

'Psalm 23 means a lot to me, "The Lord is my shepherd I shall not want…" This verse gives me strength and courage to face and overcome all difficulties. It makes me feel happiness and peace. I hope that this feeling will enrich our lives and motivate us towards peace and justice.'

Prayer

Lord, the Ethiopian on the road from Jerusalem to Gaza began to understand something of the ministry of the suffering servant. We pray for the suffering community of the Gaza Strip and pray that the seeds sown on the journey to peace may blossom and grow. Especially today we remember the Christian churches meeting in Gaza. They are our brothers and sisters in you, and we pray that you will strengthen and encourage them on their journey. Amen.

Journeying to peace
with Rabbi Jeremy Milgrom

On the road to Gaza

Rabbi Jeremy Milgrom is an American Jew from Richmond, Virginia who emigrated to Israel in 1968. He served in the army in the 1973 war and was deeply affected by the deaths of three of his friends from high school who were killed in the war and another who was injured. His first post as a rabbi was in Galilee, where many Palestinians live, and he became involved in dialogue between Jews and Palestinians. He became a parent and realized the sanctity of life. 'A child is born of a father and of a mother and of God,' he said. He decided he didn't want to carry a gun any more in the army and became active in a support group of soldiers who refused to fight in Lebanon or in the Occupied Territories during the Intifada against Palestinians.

He is the co-founder and director of a group called 'Clergy for Peace', which is an initiative for peace and justice by Muslim, Christian and Jewish clergy in Palestine and Israel. It combines dialogue and human rights activities in an effort to stimulate clergy to redefine their calling in terms of social action and to stimulate the international religious community to work for peace in the Middle East. It's an attempt to break down some of the suspicion and ignorance between the groups. He lives in Jerusalem with his three children.

I asked him for a passage of the scriptures that motivated him, and he responded with these verses from Isaiah and the following comments. 'O thou that tellest good tidings to Zion, get thee up into the high mountains, O thou that tellest good tidings to Jerusalem, lift up thy voice with strength, lift it up, be not afraid, say unto the cities of Judah, "Behold your God!"' 'Arise, shine, for thy light is come, and the glory of the Lord is risen upon thee.' (Isaiah 40:9; 60:1)—'Even though I have brought this selection in the archaic English of the libretto of Handel's *Messiah* (because the music he wrote to it is inseparable to me from these words), what my mind always reaches for is the liturgical cadence of the original Hebrew, which is read annually in the Jewish cycle of prophetic readings (Haftorah) during the wilting months of summer.

'Four summers ago, as my marriage was failing, I realized that Isaiah's encouragement for Israel addressed me as well; I found personal comfort, for the first time, in a text that I had hitherto only understood in nationalistic terms. Last week, as I travelled with a group of Israeli peace activists to Gaza to meet Chairman Arafat, the former arch-enemy of the State of Israel, still widely feared and maligned, the only tape I had in my car was that of Handel's *Messiah*; I chuckled, realizing that while I was wondering, hoping, that the aria with the above text would find new meaning in the light of our dialogue, for the more conservative among my co-religionists our meeting could not possibly be construed as "good tidings to Zion". It will be interesting to review these words with the perspective of years, and perhaps the events of the upcoming months, even weeks, could affect my judgment, but I am happy to report right now that following this visit, the prospects for peace between Israel and the Palestinians seem more positive and tangible than before. I returned home hearing new harmonies in Handel's magnificent composition, as Isaiah's timeless words of hope propelled me on my way back to Jerusalem on the wings of song, "Arise, shine, for thy light is come."'

Week Two
The Bethlehem Area

Heading south about five miles from Jerusalem on the main Hebron to Be'er Sheba road lies Bethlehem. It's quite a small town and the Church of the Nativity is, obviously, one of the most important features, built over the cave that is assumed to be the birthplace of Jesus. This is the oldest complete church in the world and to be a part of the congregation on one of the Christmas Eve celebrations here can be very moving. I say 'one' of the Christmas Eve celebrations because the Eastern Orthodox Christmas is 7 January. The site is fairly unchal-lenged as sites go. As St Jerome points out, the Emperor Hadrian, in AD135, built a grove over it, dedicated to the pagan god Adonis, with the intention of stopping Christians worshipping there. It appeared to have exactly the opposite effect as it marked the site and remained a significant place for Christians until in 315 the Emperor Constantine's mother, St Helena, directed that the basilica should be erected over the cave.

Apart from once a year, we normally don't look at the Christmas story, and we are so used to it that I think it will be valuable to look again at the manner of Jesus' birth and the stories themselves to see something of the message that maybe we don't always spot at Christmas time. There is something in the manner of the birth of the Prince of Peace that turns everything on its head. Also we'll visit the neighbouring villages of Beit Sahour (The Shepherd's Field) and a centre of hope in Beit Jala, and meet local Christian Edmund Shehadeh and, on Sunday, Palestinian Christian Saleem Munayer and Jewish Messianic believer Joseph Shulam.

A message of love
from Bethlehem

I've enjoyed visiting and doing a concert at Bethlehem Bible College. The college was established in 1979 to train Palestinian Christians to serve the Palestinian churches and ministries throughout Israel and Palestine. It is a place of fellowship and ministry to Christians from all around the globe. It is also a meeting place for the various denominations that make up the Christian rainbow here in the Holy Land. The college lies on the main road connecting Jerusalem to Hebron and it is two blocks from Rachel's Tomb, which is a historical site visited by many tourists from around the world. Bishara Awad is President and Founder of the college, a Palestinian Christian who was born in Jerusalem. After the death of his father in 1948, he was raised in a boys' orphanage in Jerusalem. Bishara has written and lectured extensively on peace and justice issues in the Middle East. He is married to Salwa Costandi Awad from Gaza and they have three grown-up children, Sami, Samir and Dina.

Bishara is a gentle and compassionate person and I asked him for his motivation and for his pointers to peace. He said, 'The cross and the love of Jesus for everybody. We Christians are to be the light and salt on this earth and spread the love of God in the midst of all the violence that is going on.' Then he quoted from 1 John 4:19–20, 'We love because he first loved us. Those who say, "I love God", and hate their brothers or sisters, are liars; for those who do not love a brother or sister whom they have seen, cannot love God whom they have not seen.' Bishara went on, 'The Bible calls us liars if we do not show love. Palestinian Christians live in the midst of turmoil and hatred where two sides are at the throats of each other—we want to be a bridge to love, a bridge to love everyone regardless, and to present the real Gospel of Jesus Christ. He died on the cross for all the world and not just for Christians and we need to spread that love to all.'

Monday of week 2
God with us

LUKE 2:1–7; MATTHEW 1:22–23

In those days a decree went out from Emperor Augustus that all the world should be registered. This was the first registration and was taken while Quirinius was governor of Syria. All went to their own towns to be registered. Joseph also went from the town of Nazareth in Galilee to Judea, to the city of David called Bethlehem, because he was descended from the house and family of David. He went to be registered with Mary, to whom he was engaged and who was expecting a child. While they were there, the time came for her to deliver her child. And she gave birth to her firstborn son and wrapped him in bands of cloth, and laid him in a manger, because there was no place for them in the inn.

All this took place to fulfil what had been spoken by the Lord through the prophet: 'Look, the virgin shall conceive and bear a son, and they shall name him Emmanuel,' which means, 'God is with us.'

Without all the resonances and romance of Christmas, maybe it is easier to come to the heart of these extraordinary words. Here is 'God with us'. God, becoming a human being—born in Bethlehem. As any pilgrim will discover, Bethlehem is an ordinary place, and this says something about the identification of God with us in our ordinary situations. According to the story, Jesus was put in a manger when he was born because they were in the place where the animals were kept—probably a cave—because there was 'no room at the inn'. Mary and Joseph—under a cloud because Mary was expecting—had made the journey from Galilee down through the Jordan valley to Bethlehem. A long and difficult journey, with Mary heavily pregnant.

I remember Malcolm Muggeridge once speculating what the situation would be if Jesus were born today and he said, 'He would have been born a Palestinian.' He said this because, for them, there is no room even in their own country. They are the most forgotten, they have been hounded from country to country as refugees—a curiously similar fate to those other children of Abraham, the Jews. For the Palestinians there is no room at the inn, even in their own society, and this birth in Bethlehem has a message of hope for them and others who are forgotten, wherever they may be—God does not forget, nor does he leave us alone.

And what does this birth in Bethlehem say for us today? It says something about the nature of God. It says something about his identification with the outcasts and the homeless. Where did God choose to meet us? Where he was not accepted, with the slur of illegitimacy and with no room in the inn and, thereby, God put a blessing for all time on the homeless and those that don't fit, and said you can meet me exactly at that point. In a world where there are a hundred million street children who have no home at all, in our own society where there are the growing numbers of homeless and those with mental illnesses on our streets, we know the attitude of God and, therefore, we know how we should respond because of the style of the birth at Bethlehem.

I sought him dressed in finest clothes
Where money talks and status grows
But power and wealth he never chose
It seemed he lived in poverty.

I sought him in the safest place
Remote from crime or cheap disgrace
But safety never knew his face
It seemed he lived in jeopardy.

I sought him where the spotlights glare
Where crowds collect and critics stare
But no one knew his presence there
It seemed he lived in obscurity.

From John L. Bell, 'Carol of the Epiphany', Iona Community

Kenneth Leech, in his book, *We Preach Christ Crucified* says, 'The cross of Christ... is a call to recognize solidarity with the Christ who has confronted pain and death once for all, and the call to minister to the wounded Christ as he is found broken and bruised on all the highways of the world. And here we see both the concrete significance and, in a profound sense, the irrelevance of Bethlehem and Calvary. Bethlehem and Calvary were the concrete, historic locations, the "sites of significance", chosen of God and precious, the redeeming places. Yet Bethlehem is wherever there is no room; Calvary is all sites of cruelty and oppression. "Just as you did it to one of the least of these... you did it to me." (Matthew 25:40).'

Thought

He did not come with wealth and grandeur.
He did not stand with men of power.
He had no status to commend him.
He was homeless, he was poor.

But he came to heal the wounded
And he came to heal the scars
Of a world that's bruised and broken,
Where the image has been marred.

And we see him in the hungry
And the homeless refugee,
In the sick and dying children
His hands reach out to you and me.

Garth Hewitt

Tuesday of week 2
'Nobodies' to 'somebodies'

LUKE 2:8-14

In that region there were shepherds living in the fields, keeping watch over their flock by night. Then an angel of the Lord stood before them, and the glory of the Lord shone around them, and they were terrified. But the angel said to them, 'Do not be afraid; for see—I am bringing you good news of great joy for all the people; to you is born this day in the city of David a Saviour, who is the Messiah, the Lord. This will be a sign for you: you will find a child wrapped in bands of cloth and lying in a manger.' And suddenly there was with the angel a multitude of the heavenly host, praising God and saying, 'Glory to God in the highest heaven, and on earth peace among those whom he favours!'

Bethlehem was known as the city of David. It was here that the young David tended the flocks of his father Jesse until he was selected by the prophet Samuel as successor to King Saul. It was here in Bethlehem that Boaz had fallen in love with Ruth and they had the son Obed, who was the father of Jesse. As we see in the family tree of Jesus in Matthew, he is in the line of David, and so it's significant that Bethlehem was his birthplace. David was the great warrior king of Israel who took Jerusalem by force and was so involved in war that he was not suitable to build a temple for the Lord. Yet his successor comes with a very different kingdom. He is to be a Prince of Peace and he will go to a throne in Jerusalem, but a very different one—that of the cross. Every step of this journey we encounter the extraordinary nature of this revolution, of the alternative values of the kingdom of God. And the message started with shepherds. Shepherds were considered the lowest of the low in those days, indeed they would virtually have been viewed as criminals. Yet it is to them that the birth of the Son of God is first announced. News of a 'Saviour' and the possibility of 'peace' is proclaimed to them, and they carry this news to Mary and Joseph. The people considered by the world to be 'nobodies' had been told by God that they are 'somebodies'. They are the first to hear of the birth of this new kind of king.

To stand overlooking the Shepherd's Field is, I think, one of the most moving sights on a journey round the Holy Land, because it is so easy to imagine that night with the shepherds out on the hillside. I remember my first night in the Holy Land occurred on 6 January—the Eastern Orthodox Christmas Eve—and so we headed out to Bethlehem. It was a shock for me to arrive in Bethlehem and to see the soldiers, and to be searched and have cameras removed from us. I hadn't realized that it was in occupied territory, and even that had a strange resonant ring. Wasn't it occupied territory once before? As we celebrated the birth of Jesus that night, armed soldiers walked between the worshippers in the Church of the Nativity in a most threatening fashion. It was a very strange feeling—and one group of people were absent—the members of the little Christian village of Beit Sahour (Shepherd's Field). The very place where the angels had sung of the possibility of 'peace on earth', could not join us that evening to celebrate the birth of the Prince of Peace. Last Christmas they held a demonstration on Christmas Eve to make the world aware that a Jewish settlement was being built on the hill overlooking their village. The hill, which they had owned for centuries, had been confiscated from them and the last Christian village in the West Bank desperately tried to make the world aware of what was happening. The demonstration worked for a time, the building was stopped but, sadly, only for a week. What does it mean for these Christians as they battle with their land being taken? The suggestion that there is a 'peace process' seems like a mockery to them. But, just as the style of the birth of the Prince of Peace tells them 'God is with you, you are not forgotten', so the message of the angels to the least in society says, 'you are not "nobodies", you are "somebodies" in the eyes of God. The world may have forgotten you, even the Christian community has forgotten you, but God has not forgotten you.'

Prayer

Lord, help us to link arms with our brothers and sisters who are forgotten, wherever they may be, knowing that this is the task of the body of Christ. And in those we meet today, may we always be sensitive to those whom life seems to push down. May we remember to be with you in lifting them up—to let the 'nobodies' be 'somebodies'. Amen.

Wednesday of week 2
The journey of the Wise Men

MATTHEW 2:1–11

In the time of King Herod, after Jesus was born in Bethlehem of Judea, wise men from the East came to Jerusalem, asking, 'Where is the child who has been born king of the Jews?...' When King Herod heard this, he was frightened, and all Jerusalem with him; and calling together all the chief priests and scribes of the people, he inquired of them where the Messiah was to be born. They told him, 'In Bethlehem of Judea...' On entering the house, they saw the child with Mary his mother; and they knelt down and paid him homage. Then, opening their treasure chests, they offered him gifts of gold, frankincense, and myrrh.

Now here comes another sign, quite a different one from the shepherds. Now we have wise men. By tradition they tend to be pictured as kings from Persia (Iran) but the Bible refers to them only as 'wise men'. They appear to be people who study the stars and were perhaps astrologers or followers of Zoroastrianism, and they follow this new star which stops over the place where Jesus was born, or where Jesus is currently living as it now appears to be a house. Is it a true story or a symbolic one? Some would say it's a 'midrash' (a story woven round a prophecy or invented to make a point) and that the early Christians included it in the nativity story. Maybe it is, but the message of it either way is very important as it's saying even kings and astrologers find their fulfilment in this baby at Bethlehem and that he's someone to be worshipped. Maybe it shows that their wisdom, which had led them to follow the star, was now superseded by another wisdom. If they were rulers, then maybe it showed that their style of kingship had been superseded by this new king, with a different, humble approach. Maybe it's symbolic, and Matthew is saying that even the rich and the powerful now bow before Jesus. It's interesting that only Luke has the shepherds and only Matthew has the wise men. Luke sees the humble and the poor being the recipients of the message of the angels, while Matthew sees the wisdom of the world bowing before this vulnerable king who will turn kingship on its head by serving.

Matthew is showing that the gospel is the gospel for all humanity. This is why, in the genealogy, at the beginning of the Gospel, he included foreigners such as Tamar, Rahab and Ruth. In 1158 three bodies were buried in Cologne Cathedral and were claimed to be those of the three wise men. It was still being used as a parable, because one of the bodies was said to be a youth, another middle-aged and the third was an old person. In paintings we find this pattern being repeated, often with one of the 'kings' being portrayed as black. So even in these ways Matthew's story that the gospel is universal, for all ages, all races, and all sections of society continues to be reflected—and the world needs to bow its head before this child.

The entrance to the Church of the Nativity is a very low doorway built by the Turks in the sixteenth century. There had been earlier doorways, some of which you can see filled in. The doors were reduced in size for reasons of defence, but for the Christian it's something of a parable, that everyone, except a child, has to bow their head in order to enter the birthplace of Jesus. Reminiscent of the words of Matthew 18:3–5, 'Unless you... become like children, you will never enter the kingdom of heaven. Whoever becomes humble like this child is the greatest in the kingdom of heaven. Whoever welcomes one such child in my name welcomes me.' The wise men had welcomed a child. God himself became a human being as a child, and we are called upon to have the humility, simplicity and perception of children.

Thought

Do we cling on to any area of superstition, even of a religious nature, that really should now be outdated because of the message of the birth of Christ?

Prayer

Thank you, scandalous God, for giving yourself to the world, not in the powerful and extraordinary, but in weakness and the familiar: in a baby; in bread and wine. Thank you for offering, at journey's end, a new beginning; for setting, in the poverty of a stable, the richest jewel of your love; the revealing, in a particular place, your light for all nations... Thank you for bringing us to Bethlehem, house of bread, where the empty are filled, and the filled are emptied; where the poor find riches, and the rich recognize their poverty; where all who kneel and hold out their hands are constantly fed.

Kate Compston from *Bread of Tomorrow*, Christian Aid

Mine eyes have seen...

LUKE 2:22–35

When the time came for their purification according to the law of Moses, they brought him up to Jerusalem to present him to the Lord... Now there was a man in Jerusalem whose name was Simeon; this man was righteous and devout, looking forward to the consolation of Israel, and the Holy Spirit rested on him... Guided by the Spirit, Simeon came into the temple; and when the parents brought in the child Jesus, to do for him what was customary under the law, Simeon took him in his arms and praised God, saying, 'Master, now you are dismissing your servant in peace, according to your word; for my eyes have seen your salvation, which you have prepared in the presence of all peoples, a light for revelation to the Gentiles and for glory to your people Israel.' And the child's father and mother were amazed at what was being said about him. Then Simeon blessed them and said to his mother Mary, 'This child is destined for the falling and the rising of many in Israel, and to be a sign that will be opposed so that the inner thoughts of many will be revealed—and a sword will pierce your own soul too.'

For Mary and Joseph it was a day out, up to Jerusalem to the temple, for the circumcision of Jesus, and while there, there was this strange encounter with a wise, old, righteous and devout man called Simeon. The interesting part of what he says is that Jesus is 'a light for revelation to the Gentiles' as well as 'glory for your people Israel'. He recognizes the universality of Christ's role. This isn't some leader of one small group of people. He glimpses that this is, in some sense, salvation for the world. Then he goes on to show something about the challenge that Jesus will bring. Just as Mary and Joseph were amazed at what he said in his blessing, then they must have been disturbed by the fact that he was to be 'a sign that will be opposed so that the inner thoughts of many will be revealed'. Maybe there's a hint here of death and resurrection—the process of following Christ is a falling and then a rising again—a losing of one's life in order to gain it.

The way of Jesus means the fall of many things that are wrong, many vested interests, and this will, inevitably, bring opposition. The road of the peacemaker is never without conflict. There are too many who have a vested interest against this pathway of peace.

Whenever I hear these words of Simeon, I am reminded of some other famous last words which seem to have a similar ring to them. On Wednesday 3 April 1968, Martin Luther King flew into Memphis, Tennessee. That night he was to deliver his last speech. He had come in to support the striking sanitation workers and in his sermon, after a masterly sweep through history, he inspires the people, gives practical advice, and then preaches about the Good Samaritan. And he ends his sermon with these words, 'But it doesn't matter with me now. Because I've been to the mountain top. And I don't mind... I just want to do God's will. And he's allowed me to go up to the mountain. And I've looked over. And I've seen the promised land. I may not get there with you. But I want you to know tonight, that we, as a people, will get to the promised land. And I'm happy, tonight. I'm not worried about anything. I'm not fearing any man. Mine eyes have seen the glory of the coming of the Lord.' 'Mine eyes have seen.' He had the clarity of vision and, perhaps, some sense of what was going to happen the next day and he was grateful that he had been able to see something of the promised land. Simeon was grateful that he had seen the one who would be the 'fulfilment of all people'. They both had a sense of fulfilment, a sense of completion.

For centuries Christians have sung the words of Simeon, 'Lord, now lettest thou thy servant depart in peace' (Nunc Dimittis). Why have we done this? Perhaps it's that deep sense of satisfaction that is expressed in Simeon in such a poetic way. He is so delighted, his whole life is fulfilled. He has met the one who will be the fulfilment of all people: 'My eyes have seen your salvation.' Simeon is satisfied. God has moved, he knew he would. Now he has seen it and all people can be satisfied in this 'light to lighten the Gentiles' and this 'glory of your people Israel'. These words have the sense of peace that a benediction (blessing) brings at the end of a service.

Prayer

Lord, may we be satisfied, like Simeon, with the salvation you have brought. May we continue to glimpse, more and more, of the height and breadth and depth of your love, as you showed it to us in Jesus Christ. Amen.

Jesus the refugee

MATTHEW 2:13–15

Now after they had left, an angel of the Lord appeared to Joseph in a dream and said, 'Get up, take the child and his mother, and flee to Egypt, and remain there until I tell you; for Herod is about to search for the child to destroy him.' Then Joseph got up, took the child and his mother by night, and went to Egypt, and remained there until the death of Herod. This was to fulfil what had been spoken by the Lord through the prophet, 'Out of Egypt I have called my son.'

Joseph was certainly prone to dreams, a bit like his namesake in the Old Testament. In Matthew's Gospel, it was in a dream that he was prompted to marry Mary even though she was already pregnant. Now Joseph is prompted in another dream to get up and flee to Egypt. So, very soon after his birth, Jesus is a refugee. In a land where so many have been turned into refugees in recent times, this is a poignant reminder that God is with us in our homelessness and in our suffering. Jesus fled *from* Bethlehem—many Palestinians fled *to* Bethlehem and to the West Bank when they were forced to leave their homes in 1948. Others fled to Lebanon and to Jordan, others to various countries around the world. Some are crowded into the most populated piece of land on earth—the Gaza Strip.

I have visited refugees fleeing from famine and from war all around the world, and when we look at the variety of problems that are causing refugees, it is good to know that we do not follow some far-off God, this is a 'God with us'—Jesus the refugee. Sometimes as we try to pray, hardly knowing what to pray for refugees from Rwanda or Bosnia, or as we hear about refugees who are victims of famine or flooding or drought, we can at least pray that Jesus the refugee, who must have a special compassion for the homeless, will go ahead of his followers in this situation, calling others to speak up or to help or to give.

The late Bishop Festo Kivengere of Uganda told me about a group of refugees for whom he campaigned, who were on the borders of Uganda and Rwanda. In fact, they were not even classified as refugees. They didn't even have that dignity, they had no status at all. They were rejected by all communities and he campaigned on their behalf to the United Nations. He told me that, as he walked around the camp, he was utterly shocked and appalled by the conditions and quite distraught, but many of the people in the camp were Christians, and they held a little service and began to sing, and the song they were singing said, 'Where God is, there is joy' and they clapped their hands and they said, 'Where God is, there is laughter' and they laughed. At first he just couldn't believe it and he went to one woman afterwards and said, 'How can you possibly praise God in this situation?' And she smiled and said to him, 'You see, Bishop, you come and visit us and then you go away again, but Jesus never leaves the camp.'

This week we are in Bethlehem and the surrounding area. Not far from Bethlehem, high on a hill, is a beacon of hope. It is the Bethlehem Arab Society for Rehabilitation in Beit Jala, which offers services to the disabled throughout the West Bank and Gaza Strip. It is a home where 'God with us' is felt very strongly. The Director is Edmund Shehadeh who is a Greek Orthodox Christian who bases his work on the belief that every human being has a right to a dignified life. By training he is a physiotherapist and his energy, determination and dedication have made this an extraordinary place. To walk around it is to hear story after story of people who otherwise would have no hope. Like Lulu who, when she was seven years old, was shot through the head by an Israeli soldier on her way home from school. Four years on, Lulu still cannot speak or hear or move, but the staff at the centre continue to give Lulu all the love and the care she needs. Others, thankfully, do improve and are able to go on and help others. Jawad, a young man who had been a victim of torture when held in prison, now runs the disabled sports section of the centre from his wheelchair and he, in turn, is an inspiration to others. You cannot leave the home without a sense of hope and without a reminder that Jesus the healer is at work today bringing hope to the wounded and the forgotten.

To think about

Take time to think of some refugee situation today, some people who the world is ignoring, someone who is homeless, someone who is disabled. Pray for them... and do something! Some small act of love, maybe write a letter on their behalf, or give something, or visit if that is a possibility. Decide on your pilgrimage to the Holy Land, you will take time to visit a home such as the one in Beit Jala.

Jesus the vulnerable child

MATTHEW 2:16–18

When Herod saw that he had been tricked by the wise men, he was infuriated, and he sent and killed all the children in and around Bethlehem who were two years old or under, according to the time that he had learned from the wise men. Then was fulfilled what had been spoken through the prophet Jeremiah: 'A voice was heard in Ramah, wailing and loud lamentation, Rachel weeping for her children; she refused to be consoled, because they are no more.'

The manner of Jesus' birth shows us so much about the heart and compassion of God. We have a story of simple people, born into poor circumstances, experiencing homelessness and refugee status. Every aspect of the story shows identification with those without a voice. This is the character of God. And as the new king is born, who asserts the value of every human being in all that he does, what is happening to the king who dominates in the local situation? He is enormously threatened and resorts, as happens so often in history, to brutality. The massacre of the innocents in Bethlehem and the neighbouring region causes weeping that cannot be comforted—just as it has in Bosnia and Rwanda. And as Mary and Joseph and the young Jesus head to Egypt, maybe they go down through Hebron, the scene of a more recent massacre, at the mosque of Abraham, where so many still cannot be comforted and they weep for those who are lost. Still the blood of God's children is shed on the land that should be the land of peace—on two wounded communities. As the Palestinians remember their massacres at the mosque of Hebron, at Sabra and Shatila up in Lebanon, or Deir Yassin in 1948, or Black September in Jordan, so too the Jews remember the fearful horrors that have happened to them through the centuries and in Auschwitz and the other camps, and Yad Vashem in Jerusalem is their poignant memorial to the attempt to eliminate them in the holocaust.

In the midst of all these massacres, is there a lesson in Herod's terrible killing of the children? Why does he do it? Why do others massacre? It's a desperate desire to cling to power or to eradicate people we fear. But the way of Jesus is a rejection of the way of Herod. We do not have to massacre any more. In Rwanda the churches—which were scenes of massacres—should have been a place of shelter because the way of Jesus is a rejection of favouring one group of people over another.

Rabbi Jonathan Sacks, in his book *Faith in the Future*, comments on Yitzhak Rabin's speech on the White House lawn at the famous shaking of hands between Rabin and Yasser Arafat. He talks about Yitzhak Rabin using a stunning example 'when he spoke about the suffering of war. He used a single image. He spoke about the pain of a land where "mothers weep for their sons."' And Jonathan Sacks goes on, 'As soon as I heard this phrase, I knew that it was a reference to the verse in Jeremiah 31:15... Rachel weeping for her sons... There were other biblical mothers who wept for their sons and I listed them. There was Hagar, who wept for Ishmael as he lay dying in the desert (Genesis 21). There was Hannah who wept for the son she could not have (1 Samuel 1). There was Sarah who, according to Rabbinic tradition, wept when she learnt that Isaac was about to be offered as a sacrifice (Genesis 22). There was the mother of Sisera who wept when her son was killed in battle against the Israelites (Judges 5). With a shock of recognition, I realised that these five texts were connected. The peace agreement with the Palestinians was concluded three days before the Jewish New Year. Four of the texts were taken from the bibical readings for the New Year. The fifth is the symbolism behind the festival's great religious act, the blowing of the ram's horn. It's sound, says the Talmud, is meant to represent the weeping of the mother of Sisera... On the Jewish New Year we remember the tears shed not only for Israel, but also for Israel's rivals, Ishmael and Sisera.' We have to recognize our common humanity and recognize our common pain.

In our world at the moment there are a hundred million street kids for whom no one cares. Children are faced with war and with hunger and, if God is with the homeless, he is also with the child on the streets of Manila or Mozambique or Brazil or Peru. The massacre of the children goes on now in other ways where, in their poverty, they are exploited, for instance, in the sex trade. Maybe even Herod would have balked at this, and the example of people like Father Shay Cullen in the Phillipines as he fights to have Western tourists and military people brought to court for these crimes against children is a work of profound importance because it asserts that God is not on the side of Herod but on the side of abused and forgotten children. The innocents are being massacred on the streets of our world today. The body of Christ are to be those who say 'no' to the ways of Herod and 'yes' to reaching out to the children.

Prayer

Lord, remove from us any of the ways of Herod. Instead, may we follow the way of Jesus, the way of humility and non-violence, the way of healing and hope. Amen.

Peter at Joppa

ACTS 10:1–15

In Caesarea there was a man named Cornelius... he had a vision in which he saw an angel of God coming in and saying... 'Send men to Joppa for a certain Simon who is called Peter; he is lodging with Simon, a tanner, whose house is by the seaside.'... About noon the next day... Peter went up on the roof to pray. He became hungry and wanted something to eat; and while it was being prepared, he fell into a trance. He saw the heaven opened and something like a large sheet coming down, being lowered to the ground by its four corners. In it were all kinds of four-footed creatures and reptiles and birds of the air. Then he heard a voice saying, 'Get up, Peter; kill and eat.' But Peter said, 'By no means, Lord; for I have never eaten anything that is profane or unclean.' The voice said to him again, a second time, 'What God has made clean, you must not call profane.'

Here we are on the coast at Joppa, just south of modern-day Tel Aviv, in what is now called Jaffa. Peter, we know from the end of Acts 9, had stayed some time in Joppa, at the house of Simon the tanner. This is particularly significant because a tanner was involved in treating the skins of dead animals, thus in contact with what is unclean according to Jewish Law, so many would have despised him. Peter's decision to stay with him shows that already he is rejecting the old prejudice and this prepares him for the vision that now comes.

It is a vision of enormous significance as it breaks down the old restrictions of the past and makes God a God who is inclusive rather than exclusive. The vision has prepared Peter to go up to Caesarea to meet Cornelius—a Gentile—and his friends. And in his sermon up there, he recognizes that God shows no partiality, but in every nation, anyone who fears him and does what is right is acceptable to him. So this is an important moment for the new Church as they are told the barriers are coming down in the new kingdom.

Sadly, last year in Jaffa a soldier from the Israeli defence force called Shanial Koren entered the church of St Anthony on a Monday evening and opened fire indiscriminately, in a scene reminiscent of the Hebron mosque shooting. Though no injuries were reported, the church suffered extensive damage and it was a considerable shock to the Christians of Jaffa. An incident such as this tries to keep up walls of division, but people of good will need to work to bring them down.

One such group is 'Musalaha'. This is a ministry of reconciliation between Palestinian Christians and Messianic Jews who are working together trying to face the realities of living in a region that is divided, yet they know that their gospel says this should not be the case. Saleem Munayer, who founded Musalaha, says they have in common 'the fundamental belief that we are all created in God's image and that through his love the wall of hatred and enmity must be broken down. Our belief in Jesus as the Messiah is the foundation for our gathering and reconciliation. We do acknowledge our efforts are small in comparison to the magnitude of the issues facing the two peoples who are living in this land. But we have faith that, as a result of our obedience, our small step of love may change the course of history for our people.' The word 'musalaha' is an Arabic word which means forgiveness and reconciliation and this group tries, in various ways, to break down the barrier between Palestinian and Jew. One way has been a journey into the wilderness together, where they spent time getting to know each other and praying together.

Joseph Shulam, who is pastor of Netivyah Messianic Jewish community and one of Musalaha's board members, says, 'The concept of reconciliation is one of the major themes of the whole Bible. From the day that Adam and Eve were thrown out of the garden, God's will has always been to reconcile all men unto himself... The situation is that we are saturated with hatred, enmity and violence on all sides, and that either as Israelis or Palestinians, as Jews or as Arabs, we are pulled apart by our compatriots.' He goes on to say, 'You can never reconcile two sides who both think that they are absolutely right and that the other side is absolutely wrong... If you want to reconcile, the first thing you have to realize is that you must be humble... so reconciliation has to be willing to admit faults.'

Blood Brothers

When will the children of Abraham find their peace?

Blood brothers, with the same plea:
'Give us a land where we can be free.'
Blood brothers, with a wounded past,
How long must your sorrow last—
Will it last—must it last?

Does it have to be this way?
Soldier, throw that gun away.
From Galilee came a man,
He shed his blood upon this land,
Pouring peace from wounded hands.

When will the children of Abraham find their peace?

Blood brothers, in the same land;
With the same father—Abraham,
You are Jew and Palestinian;
Will you ever walk hand in hand—
Hand in hand—make a Holy Land?

When will the children of Abraham find their peace?

To think about

Are there walls of division in your life that need bringing down? Jesus
calls us all to be peacemakers. Are there people from whom you are
separated, are there relationships that need to be restored? Take time
to be quiet and think, and see if God is asking you to take some steps
towards practical reconciliation.

Nazareth and Capernaum

Now we have headed back up to Nazareth and during this week we will be based in Nazareth, moving out to Cana and then to Capernaum by the Sea of Galilee.

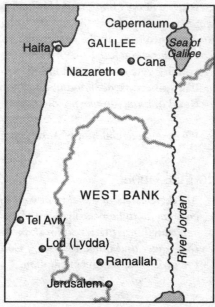

My host in Nazareth has always been my close friend Archdeacon Riah Abu El-Assal, who is also Vicar of Christ Church. He and other Christians from his church, and from the other churches, have given me a great welcome, and I have met up with Catholics, Baptists and Orthodox. Can any good come from Nazareth? Well, obviously the Anglican Church thinks it can because he has been elected the new Bishop in the Jerusalem diocese. Riah and his family are extremely warm-hearted and when I was touring with him in the UK on one occasion, the *Church Times* described him as 'an Archdeacon you can hug'. No doubt now, he will be a Bishop you can hug!

Riah was born in Nazareth in 1937 but in 1948 the family were in Lebanon and were refused the right to return. They did return in 1949—on foot across the border and their status was illegal until 1958. Riah married Suad and has a son Hanna, and daughters Lorraine and Rania. He was a founding member of the Nazareth Democratic Front, the Committee for the Defence of Arab Land, and the Progressive Movement in Nazareth. He was Secretary General of the Progressive List for Peace, and he was number three on the list of candidates for the Knesset in 1984 and 1988 (two were elected). In 1985 he was a member of a six man Israeli delegation—three Jews and three Arabs—to Tunis to meet with Chairman Arafat of the PLO, and from August 1986 to January 1990 was banned from travel abroad for which no explanation was given and no charges made. In April 1994 the South African Department of

Foreign Affairs welcomed him as part of an official fact-finding mission to South Africa. On 12 June 1995 he was elected co-adjutor Bishop to the Diocese of Jerusalem.

If you look up Nazareth in tourist books you don't find anything too hopeful about it, even today. I quote from one of them. When it comes to Nazareth, it says, 'Home of Mary and Joseph and the town where Jesus was brought up, has a name as resonant as any in Israel. Expect to be disappointed. For all the churches and Christian shrines which mark out the New Testament story, this is not an appealing city: underfunded, overcrowded and choked with traffic... You should still visit, of course... but it really doesn't need a great deal of time.' Yes, do visit and the good you'll find in Nazareth lies in people rather than old stones. It is the largest Palestinian city in Israel and many would still say, 'Can any good come out of Nazareth?' Take time to discover its 'good' by meeting the 'living stones'.

Back to Nazareth

LUKE 2:39–40; MATTHEW 2:19–23

When they had finished everything required by the law of the Lord, they returned to Galilee, to their own town of Nazareth. The child grew and became strong, filled with wisdom; and the favour of God was upon him.

When Herod died, an angel of the Lord suddenly appeared in a dream to Joseph in Egypt and said, 'Get up, take the child and his mother, and go to the land of Israel, for those who were seeking the child's life are dead.' Then Joseph got up, took the child and his mother, and went to the land of Israel. But when he heard that Archelaus was ruling over Judea in place of his father Herod, he was afraid to go there. And after being warned in a dream, he went away to the district of Galilee. There he made his home in a town called Nazareth, so that what had been spoken through the prophets might be fulfilled, 'He will be called a Nazorean.'

Here we find some differences in the stories of Matthew and Luke but one thing they have in common is that Mary and Joseph and Jesus went to—or returned to—Nazareth. In Luke, it's a return because they had been up in Nazareth before and had gone down to Bethlehem because of the census. In Matthew, Nazareth hasn't been mentioned before and he seems to give the impression that they would have gone back to Bethlehem but instead, because they were afraid of Archelaus, they headed up into Galilee, to Nazareth, and this fulfilled prophecy. Matthew is always concerned that Jesus should be seen as the Messiah, as a fulfilment of prophecy and he has, when he is writing, a particular eye to the Jewish constituency so that they will be convinced. Luke's story seems to be that of an insider more than a theological interpretation. Perhaps he gleaned it from Mary—the mother of Jesus. Anyway, the whole story has shifted to Galilee, and to Nazareth, where the child grows up, and we have little information apart from the fact that he was wise and God's blessing was upon him.

In Luke's Gospel, the next story has them rushing off to Jerusalem again for the Passover Festival. However, Jesus was twelve at this time, so there's been a considerable gap and both today's passage and the passage when he goes to Jerusalem remind us that he grew in wisdom and also, it adds, 'in divine and human favour'. People liked Jesus. He was an ordinary lad, his humanity would have shone out. They didn't go around saying, 'Oh, that's the Son of God.' People would not have been aware of his significance until the time of his ministry when he began to make it clear.

Matthew again had Joseph dreaming, and Joseph dreaming in Egypt has an Old Testament resonance to it. As a result of the dream, the refugees headed home. It's from this home that Jesus' ministry will begin, many years' later. What sort of an upbringing was it? Well, the Bible is silent but, one thing is for sure, it would have been normal. Jesus wasn't thought of as a particularly religious child. The incident in the temple seems to suggest that he would have been thought of as bright and wise but when, in later years, he speaks in the synagogue at Nazareth, they are surprised and say, 'Isn't this Jesus, the son of Joseph?' It seems, therefore, that he grew up without a lot of pressure put on him, without high expectations. Sometimes in Christian homes children are expected to develop spirituality very early. The parents are constantly looking to see how the Christianity is displayed. Maybe if they were simply taught the Christian way and allowed to develop themselves, it would be more the way Jesus was brought up. Certainly he would have learnt week by week at the synagogue and so too it's good for children of Christian homes to learn the basics of the faith, but not to be expected to show great spirituality too early.

After the journey to Jerusalem, at the age of twelve, we don't see Jesus until eighteen years later. What was he doing? Presumably working in his father's workshop, working with his hands, making things out of wood. We don't know when Joseph died, but it was before Jesus' ministry, so maybe he had to take the work over and be able to keep Mary and his family. But all the time he was learning, growing in wisdom and getting ready for that time when he would reveal the significance of his ministry.

Prayer

Lord, may we grow steadily in our understanding of you, in our understanding of the world, and in our understanding of ourselves, and may we grow in favour with you and with others as we follow the path you have shown us. In your name. Amen.

Can any good come from Nazareth?

JOHN 1:43-47

The next day Jesus decided to go to Galilee. He found Philip and said to him, 'Follow me.' Now Philip was from Bethsaida, the city of Andrew and Peter. Philip found Nathanael and said to him, 'We have found him about whom Moses wrote in the law and also the prophets wrote, Jesus son of Joseph from Nazareth.' Nathanael said to him, 'Can anything good come out of Nazareth?' Philip said to him, 'Come and see.' When Jesus saw Nathanael coming toward him, he said of him, 'Here is truly an Israelite in whom there is no deceit!'

This story comes early in John's Gospel, and it's interesting because it gives an insight into the way in which people from Nazareth were viewed. Nathanael, who only came from a few miles away (Cana) obviously voiced the local prejudice that no good could come from Nazareth. This seems to fit in with the pattern that we've already seen about the manner of Jesus' birth, identifying with the poor and the homeless, people who are not viewed as if they are of great significance in the eyes of the world. And here is Jesus, being brought up in a small town that is thought of as nowhere. We can all think of places like this; maybe we think we live in one, maybe we're wondering what's the point of being here. We're off the map, and yet being off the map can be a place that is very significant in the eyes of God.

Nazareth was a humble place and it still is today. All the tourists tend to go and stay in Tiberias and spend only a few minutes in Nazareth, but there is nothing more rewarding than staying longer and meeting the local 'living stones'. This is the way the Christians of the Holy Land describe themselves—they see millions of Christians from all around the world come to visit their land and, in their busy schedules, they leap in and out of their coaches and look at all sorts of old stones. They keep in a huddle together, they pray together, and sing together, and even have the communion together, but it's in a circle. It doesn't open up and reach out to the 'living stones', to the local Christian community, and they've been deeply hurt by all of this. It's as if they don't exist. Can any good come out of Nazareth? Oh yes, and it still does.

I was on a tour in Poland a few years back and I was playing towns that everyone had heard of such as Warsaw and Krakow, and at the end of the tour details it mentioned one little place that no one seemed to have heard of. It was a place called Zelow, and the tour was advertised on television and everyone kept saying, 'Where is Zelow?' In fact, Zelow is on the edge of the biggest ecological scar in Europe, a huge area which has been strip-mined, destroying villages and communities. And Zelow, perched on the end of this, feels like it's at the end of the world, miles away from anyone. No one visits it and they feel forgotten. When the local Communist leader saw the advertising, he came to the people of the church and said, 'Surely he'll not visit Zelow? No one visits Zelow.' And everyone kept coming up to the people who were organizing the concert and saying, 'He won't come to Zelow.' When I arrived there, I got the most incredible welcome and the pastor said to me, 'You see, people feel no one comes to Zelow, not even Christ would come to Zelow and sometimes I even feel that and I have to remind myself that he is with us, even at the end of the world.'

I had arrived there very tired and wondering why on earth we were going there and, of course, it was the most significant concert of the tour. Everyone from the local community crowded into the little church. Can any good come from Zelow? Of course it can. They may be forgotten, they may be hurt and wounded, but they're a community who have had to rebuild themselves against all odds. The spirituality and warmth and strength of these people made me think of it as a little Nazareth. Forgotten by the world, but not forgotten by God.

Thought

Maybe you live in a Nazareth or a Zelow, or you think of it that way. Or maybe you think of some other areas in that way. Or perhaps God is calling you to live in an area that you view that way. Let this story remind you to see places through God's eyes and to recognize their potential and to see people in the same way. Jesus saw huge potential in Nathanael. He compared him to Jacob (Israel), who was known as 'a man of guile'. Jesus saw Nathanael as an Israelite without guile or deceit. Pray that today you will see the potential in those that you meet, ask for forgiveness for any you have knowingly put down or have felt are of no significance.

From ordinary water to joyful wine

JOHN 2:1–11

On the third day there was a wedding in Cana of Galilee, and the mother of Jesus was there. Jesus and his disciples had also been invited to the wedding. When the wine gave out, the mother of Jesus said to him, 'They have no wine.' And Jesus said to her, 'Woman, what concern is that to you and me? My hour has not yet come.' His mother said to the servants, 'Do whatever he tells you.' Now standing there were six stone water jars for the Jewish rites of purification, each holding twenty or thirty gallons. Jesus said to them, 'Fill the jars with water.'... The steward called the bridegroom and said to him, 'Everyone serves the good wine first, and then the inferior wine after the guests have become drunk. But you have kept the good wine until now.' Jesus did this, the first of his signs, in Cana of Galilee and revealed his glory.

Today we journey to Cana. It's about five miles north-east of Nazareth on the road to Tiberias. It's the scene of Jesus' first miracle. The dialogue between him and his mother is almost amusing, as he appears rather abruptly to tell her he is not ready to embark on his ministry. She, obviously, takes no notice of this and assumes that he will help out with the situation. At this point, the story becomes very symbolic as John uses the six stone water jars for the Jewish rites of purification in order to make a theological point. If Jesus really did turn 120 to 180 gallons of water into wine, after people had already drunk well, then this must have been a truly remarkable wedding feast! This passage, though, is not so much concerned with the quantity of wine but, rather, the point that John is making. The water jars stand for the Jewish rites of the old covenant and right at the beginning of his ministry, Jesus is showing that the new covenant is like good wine, whereas the old covenant is like water in comparison. This new covenant, this kingdom of God, is really good wine and everything else pales into insignificance beside it.

Nathanael came from Cana of Galilee (John 21:2), which explains the rivalry that we saw yesterday with his comment, 'Can any good come from Nazareth?' Today many visitors might be tempted to say, 'Can any good come from Cana?' Cana is a mixed Christian and Muslim village with a population of around 10,000. They are traditionally farmers but much of their land has been confiscated and so the remaining land can no longer support the villagers. After the confiscations in 1976, protest demonstrations erupted in many villages in Galilee. In Cana, a fifteen-year-old boy, Mehsin Hassan Taha, was killed by Israeli soldiers. His death, and the death of the others that occurred at this time in other Galilee villages, is remembered each year on Land Day, 30 March. The guide books are equally rude about Cana as they are about Nazareth. Once again the temptation might be not to visit it, because it doesn't look so great, but let's not forget the people of this community. Jesus would not only want us to look at the history but also their story and their sufferings.

Thought

Jesus comes to transform situations. There may be something in your life that seems so ordinary—it's water that needs to be transformed. Sit and think about it and consider what would it look like, as Jesus turns it into wine, as that situation is filled with hope and joy.

Prayer

You have kept the good wine until now; the wine that we have longed for, but never thought to taste. You have taken the tap water of our lives, our struggles and our ordinariness, and with your grace made sweet and dark and heady all that our hearts contain. So also take the dreams of both your beloved peoples in this, your Holy Land, and make them dance, that all the world may come to join in celebration.

Janet Morley, in *Companions of God*, Christian Aid

Good news to the poor

LUKE 4:16–21

When he came to Nazareth, where he had been brought up, he went to the synagogue on the sabbath day, as was his custom. He stood up to read, and the scroll of the prophet Isaiah was given to him. He unrolled the scroll and found the place where it was written: 'The Spirit of the Lord is upon me, because he has anointed me to bring good news to the poor. He has sent me to proclaim release to the captives and recovery of sight to the blind, to let the oppressed go free, to proclaim the year of the Lord's favour.' And he rolled up the scroll, gave it back to the attendant, and sat down. The eyes of all in the synagogue were fixed on him. Then he began to say to them, 'Today this scripture has been fulfilled in your hearing.'

In Christ Church, Nazareth, behind the altar, there are words written in Arabic script. They are very beautiful and there is added poignancy when one realizes it is these words that Jesus spoke in the synagogue at Nazareth. He speaks these words right at the beginning of his ministry, from Isaiah chapter 61, and it puts Jesus firmly in the tradition of what the prophet Isaiah promised of the one who brings peace and establishes justice. One day Archdeacon Riah took us just down the road from Christ Church to a little old synagogue that some say stands on the site of the synagogue of Our Lord's time, and here Riah talked about these wonderful words that set the tone of the ministry of Jesus. Somehow, sitting in that little old synagogue, as we read afresh those words, it seemed to bring alive that commitment to the poor and to the oppressed. We've seen how the manner of Jesus' birth identified with the homeless and the refugee and the powerless, and now we see him echo this as he describes his ministry for the first time. This has been called the 'Nazareth manifesto' as Jesus sets out the values of the upside-down kingdom, which are so clearly embedded in the prophets of the Jewish scriptures.

In Luke's Gospel, Jesus first announces his ministry in terms of 'good news to the poor'. Luke has a particular compassion for the poor and for the forgotten. The coming of the kingdom of God is seen in terms of righting the wrongs of society—a kingdom that lifts up the fallen, that sets free the oppressed and, of course, as Mary's song reminds us, not only lifts up those who are considered lowly but brings down the mighty from their seats. Why? Just to humiliate them? No, in order that they, too, can be set free from their oppression—their oppression of dominating and manipulating. This two-edged sword of a gospel, in the end, brings hope for everyone, but not always in the ways we would expect. The poor are valued and offered hope, but only because we in the affluent West—the rich and the powerful—are offered the opportunity to lose our lives in order that we may gain them.

I asked Riah what was his favourite verse of the Bible and, also, what were his hopes for peace. I wasn't surprised when he replied, 'Luke 4:18 is my favourite verse. It is the only thing left in Christ Church from the first decoration of our church building. You remember the writing on the wall behind the altar. Though I know it caused a lot of trouble for Jesus in those days, it has continued to influence my life, my thinking and to help shape my ministry over the last thirty years.

'The "good news to the poor" is related to the ultimate reign of justice and peace in our world where the majority of the masses are of that category [poor]. "Release to the prisoners" did not speak only of those in prisons or detained or under occupation but also those prisoners of fear, of guilt, of shame, and the like. "Recovery of sight" had more to do with sharing the truth, the very facts about a certain situation, such as the one in the Middle East with the many who were blind and ignorant and therefore indifferent to the cries of the oppressed. And finally the healing ministry of the broken - hearted—and such are millions around us: the refugees, the homeless, the detained, those who have lost dear ones, the dispossessed of their home countries, and those who have lost hope and faith in him who is able to heal their wounds and wipe out their tears.'

Prayer

Lord, here we are in Nazareth—the town of your formative years.
And the wonderful words of this Nazareth mandate go down through
the centuries and remind us of the tasks of the kingdom of God and
the hope of the kingdom of God. We ask that we will be people of your
kingdom, and walk your road with you. Amen.

Friday of week 3
The birth of Jesus foretold at Nazareth

LUKE 1:26–33

In the sixth month the angel Gabriel was sent by God to a town in Galilee called Nazareth, to a virgin engaged to a man whose name was Joseph, of the house of David. The virgin's name was Mary. And he came to her and said, 'Greetings, favoured one! The Lord is with you.' But she was much perplexed by his words and pondered what sort of greeting this might be. The angel said to her, 'Do not be afraid, Mary, for you have found favour with God. And now, you will conceive in your womb and bear a son, and you will name him Jesus. He will be great, and will be called the Son of the Most High, and the Lord God will give to him the throne of his ancestor David. He will reign over the house of Jacob forever, and of his kingdom there will be no end.'

Any pilgrim to Nazareth will be rushed to the Church of the Annunciation because, obviously, this is one of the key reasons why Nazareth is on the tourist map. The angel Gabriel came to Mary and told her that she would conceive, and told her something of the nature of this unusual child whose kingdom would have no end. Her simple obedience has been an example throughout the centuries.

One day Riah took me over the road from Christ Church and down underneath the Catholic convent belonging to the Sisters of Nazareth. Underneath is an ancient house, which gives an idea of the sort of place in which Mary would have been living. Nearby is also a tomb with a stone that can be rolled across, very like the Garden Tomb in Jerusalem. Here you can sit and look at the house and imagine old Nazareth as it must have been at the time when Mary was living here. Then a short stroll down the road brings you to the huge Basilica of the Annunciation which the Catholics have built. This is on the top of a house which is claimed to be part of the home of Mary and the Basilica is the fifth building to have been erected on this spot. It's impressive and it's striking, with decorative panels from all around the world and some fine stained glass windows, but I don't necessarily find that I can

56

imagine the annunciation so well here as I could sitting quietly by the other little house. Perhaps that house and the old synagogue are the places that I found most significant in Nazareth. The annunciation story itself continues the pattern that we have already noticed. Mary comments how God has looked with favour on the lowliness of his servant. This was a humble community, a humble house, a humble person and now, already, before Christ is born we see a lifting up of the lowly. And in the confusion of Herod we will see the rich being sent empty away.

The tourist guides tell us that Nazareth is not a place to stop long. It is a town which is dominated by the Basilica. But when I go to Nazareth, I slip up the hill to Christ Church to see the wonderful work they are doing in the school there with the children. I am sung to by the children with such power and joy, and I take time to worship with the community there. All this reminds me that often those who are just off the map can refresh us in ways we never expect. This is part of the message of the upside-down kingdom. Riah is one of the peacemakers that we come to value on our journey, a person who has allowed the joy of his Christian faith to influence his whole life and his struggle for his own people.

Riah comments, 'For anyone who endeavours to implement the mind of Christ, they will have a similar fortune to Christ. They wanted to hurl Jesus over the hill but he managed to escape their anger for a while. In my case they tried to defame me, to trap me, to control my movements, to humiliate me, all with the intention of crushing my spirit. But by the grace of God I managed to stand firm in my convictions, and kept up the struggle for peace, for justice and for reconciliation. I claim no credit. People are changing. Realities are being recognized. And I confess that one of my weaknesses, if you want to describe it that way, is that I cannot give up my optimism. And I strongly believe victory is on the side of all that safeguards the image of God in human beings.'

Walk In His Shoes

He's a friend of the poor, he brings good news;
A friend of the oppressed, he walks in their shoes.
He hungers for justice for those born to lose.
He's the healer of the broken, confused and abused,
and those of us who follow him must walk in his shoes.

Garth Hewitt

Jesus moves to Capernaum

MATTHEW 4:12–17

Now when Jesus heard that John had been arrested, he withdrew to Galilee. He left Nazareth and made his home in Capernaum by the sea, in the territory of Zebulun and Naphtali, so that what had been spoken through the prophet Isaiah might be fulfilled: 'Land of Zebulun, land of Naphtali, on the road by the sea, across the Jordan, Galilee of the Gentiles—the people who sat in darkness have seen a great light, and for those who sat in the region and shadow of death light has dawned.' From that time Jesus began to proclaim, 'Repent, for the kingdom of heaven has come near.'

Jesus hears the news John's arrest and he moves from Nazareth to Galilee. It seems there are two possible reasons for this. First, the sense that now John's ministry is finished and his must begin; and secondly, that Nazareth was perhaps too close to the government centre of Sepphoris. So it may have been a move for greater safety, to enable him to take up his work without interference.

Matthew uses the old Israelite tribal names of Zebulun and Naphtali (Capernaum is in Naphtali) even though they had fallen out of use in his day, because he is wanting to defend the Messiah being in this rather unexpected place rather than in the religious capital Jerusalem or in the desert. The word that's used here, for making his home in Capernaum, is the verb *katoikein* and this implies actually acquiring a house in Capernaum. It was the base from which Jesus was going to operate, based on the north-west bank of the Sea of Galilee and with easy access to escape by sea across to the area of Decapolis. It gave him mobility.

Matthew quotes from the wonderful passage at the beginning of Isaiah 9. There are not many references to Galilee in the Old Testament and this one is perhaps the best known, particularly because of the phrase 'Galilee of the nations'. The area was surrounded on three sides by non-Jewish populations, hence the reference to the nations, and under the Maccabees the Gentile influence on the Jews had been so strong that for half a century the Jews had withdrawn further south. So Galilee had had to be re-colonized. Because of this, and because of the fact that its population was very diverse, the Galileans were often treated with contempt by Jews from the south. There's almost a sort of racism about Galilee which we see expressed in John 7:52 when the Pharisees say to Nicodemus, 'Surely you are not also from Galilee, are you? Search and you will see that no prophet is to arise from Galilee.' Matthew is making it clear that there is hope for Galilee, as it says in Isaiah 9, 'In the latter time he will make glorious the way of the sea, the land beyond the Jordan, Galilee of the nations.' Matthew is at pains to make it clear that Jesus is the fulfilment of this and so 'the people who walked in darkness have seen a great light…'.

In verse 16, Matthew seems to mix the quote in Isaiah 9 with a passage in Isaiah 42:6–7 which talks about the people who sit in darkness. The passage says, 'I have given you as a covenant to the people, a light to the nations, to open the eyes that are blind, to bring out the prisoners from the dungeon, from the prison those who sit in darkness.' So, in this passage at the beginning of the ministry of Jesus in Matthew, there are echoes of what Luke brings out in the synagogue at Nazareth, where Luke is also quoting from Isaiah.

Luke also quotes from Isaiah about the ministry of John the Baptist saying that he was 'the voice of one crying out in the wilderness: "Prepare the way of the Lord, make his path straight. Every valley shall be filled, and every mountain and hill shall be made low, and the crooked shall be made straight, and the rough ways made smooth; and all flesh shall see the salvation of God."' So we see in both Luke and Matthew that this new kingdom that's coming will not have great inequalities. There will be a 'making straight' of society, the imbalances will disappear, the valleys will be filled in and the mountains brought low, then 'the glory of the Lord shall be revealed'.

Have we somehow lost the excitement of this new kingdom, and the way it should change society and bring hope? Are we even frightened of it? What message does it have for the present day? Do we believe it would work in Britain, in your town and in mine?

It certainly has a significant message within the land where Jesus walked. The gospel says the valleys will be lifted up and the hills brought down. The people who are considered as nothing—to be pushed out and to be trampled on—are to be treasured, the gospel says. The people who are dominating and abusing will be brought low. How low? Will they be trampled lower than the other people? No, this is not the gospel. The gospel says the rich and the powerful will be brought low, so they are at the same level as the others who are brought up. The valleys are filled in and the mountains are brought low. So no one is destroyed. Ironically, the oppressor finds freedom to be treated equally like the person who used to be oppressed. The successor to the warrior king is the peace king, the one who makes society straight and those of us who are members of the Body of Christ have the same task, to fill in the valleys, to bring down the mountains.

Thought

Try and list, in our society, valleys that need to be filled in and mountains that need to be brought low. What would make our society reflect the values of the kingdom of God? How should the body of Christ—the Church—play its part in this?

Peter in Lydda (Lod)

ACTS 9:32–35

Now as Peter went here and there among all the believers, he came down also to the saints living in Lydda. There he found a man named Aeneas, who had been bed-ridden for eight years, for he was paralysed. Peter said to him, 'Aeneas, Jesus Christ heals you; get up and make your bed!' And immediately he got up. And all the residents of Lydda and Sharon saw him and turned to the Lord.

Here in Lydda there is already a group of believers and Aeneas is one of this fellowship. Peter heals him very much in the style of Jesus—the works of Jesus the healer are carried on by the apostles and an incident like this resulted in many others becoming followers.

There has been a community of Christians in Lydda ever since this. Audeh Rantisi can trace his family, through church records and oral tradition, back to the fourth century. He even wonders if his family became Christians the day Aeneas was healed! Lydda had been one of the most prosperous Arab towns in the country, but in 1948 most of the Palestinians were driven out. Audeh was eleven at the time and speaks graphically in his book *Blessed Are The Peacemakers* about his memory of that occasion.

I cannot forget three horror-filled days in July of 1948... First Israeli soldiers forced thousands of Palestinians from their homes... then, without water, we stumbled into the hills and continued for three deadly days. The Jewish soldiers followed, occasionally shooting over our heads to scare us and keep us moving. The soldiers stopped us and ordered everyone to throw all valuables on to a blanket. One young man and his wife of six weeks, friends of our family, stood near me. He refused to give up his money. Almost casually, the soldier pulled up his rifle and shot the man. He fell, bleeding and dying, while his bride screamed and cried. I felt nauseated and sick, my whole body numbed by shock-waves. That night I cried too, as I tried to sleep alongside thousands on the ground. Would I ever see my home again?

Eventually they ended up as refugees in Ramallah, ten miles from Jerusalem. Four years after these painful events, Audeh dedicated his life to the service of Jesus Christ. It was the famous verse, John 3:16, 'For God so loved the world...' that got through to him and he says, 'It was through this verse that the Lord brought me into a personal relationship with him, as a young man. ... Here is a love that gives, a love that forgives, a love that accepts at face value.'

Audeh talks also about how this same verse prompted him in his vocation later on, 'It was one Sunday afternoon, going on a walk, that this verse came to me again. It was through this that I experienced my peace with God and my calling into full-time service. In my case, this led to founding and directing a boys' home for deprived Palestinian children.' Over the years, over 200 boys have been cared for in this home. Audeh, the man from Lydda, is another who could have been a bitter person. Instead, he has dedicated his life to showing love in action. Not only has he run the Evangelical Boys' Home in Ramallah with his wife, Patricia, but also he stood for local political office, 'When asked to run for municipal elections in 1976 I questioned "why" but the Lord had a reason. I experienced a presence and peace of the Lord in the most dark and difficult situations, and the Lord enabled me to share his message of salvation and peace during the most turbulent days. People were challenged, comforted and strengthened and the municipal office became a pulpit to share the Lord's love and concern to the Palestinian people.'

Modern Lydda has almost 40,000 residents, of whom only 5,000 are Palestinians. The present Greek Orthodox church was built a little over 100 years ago on the site of churches dating back to the sixth century and has the tomb of England's patron saint, St George, with a portrait of him slaying the dragon. This is not exactly a tourist site for English pilgrims, and it seems we are a little mystified as to why St George is our patron saint! It's interesting to note that our patron saint is a Palestinian and no doubt there will be controversy as to exactly where he is buried or, indeed, exactly who he was. Presumably his story was brought back by the crusaders.

Next to St George's Orthodox Church is St George's Episcopal Church, where Zahi Nassir is the vicar. He is also the chaplain of Tabeetha School in Jaffa. Zahi and Muna and their children live here and carry on their work in the local community.

Thought

Peter came to Lydda and then moved on to carry on his ministry. Audeh was forcibly moved from Lydda and has carried on his ministry in Ramallah. Zahi came from Nazareth to carry on his ministry in Lod. All on a journey, sometimes as pilgrims, sometimes as refugees, but living the gospel wherever they find themselves. Pray today for the churches meeting in Lod and in Ramallah.

From Nazareth to Lod

Zahi speaks about his faith and motivation, 'Peace, for me, is not only the absence of armed struggle and wars and violent acts. Peace is the quality of life we live—the life that God had intended to give us as a gift for all human beings. Peace is a life lived fully in respect of other human beings and in adoration and worship of God. Peace, I believe, is when I am sure that my fellow human being goes to sleep every night with his family, in happiness and contentment. It is when I am certain that there is no one in a prison camp because of his struggle for freedom and to be treated as a respected human being.

'Peace means the life when "we and they" are free from being paranoid and antagonistic towards each other... Peace and oppression, peace and occupation, cannot go hand in hand. Peace is to live the life fully with everybody and with God in love.' And the passage of the Bible that particularly inspires Zahi is Luke 4:16–19, 'The Spirit of the Lord is upon me...', the Nazareth manifesto—which is not surprising because Zahi originates from Nazareth!

Week Four
Galilee

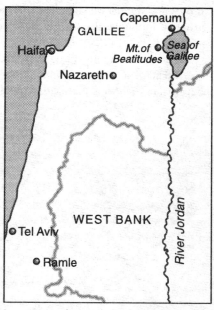

Now Jesus has moved to Capernaum, we will stay in Galilee this week and next week as we follow him around, teaching, telling parables and doing miracles. In Matthew's Gospel, he has just called his first disciples, Simon Peter and Andrew, who were probably fairly successful fishermen. He said to them, 'Follow me, and I will make you fish for people.' In verse 20 of Matthew 4 it says, '*Immediately* they left their nets and followed him.' Presumably this was not their first meeting with Jesus and no doubt there was something about him that already impressed them but, nevertheless, this is a very decisive move. The words 'follow me' that are used in verse 19 suggest the technical language of a teacher to disciples, yet it would be unusual for a teacher to take the initiative. Jesus received prompt response—just as he expects later in Matthew's Gospel when someone asks to go and bury his father. Jesus responds, 'Follow me, and let the dead bury their own dead.' Obviously the story may have suffered from being edited heavily by Matthew.

This is a major decision for Simon and Andrew and, no doubt, is the culmination of some thinking and discussing rather than a sudden and irrational response to a passing stranger. It is as if Jesus has already had contact with them and now is going to round them up, because from here he goes on to James and John, the sons of Zebedee, and they also immediately leave the boat and their father and follow him. Now we discover from Matthew that Jesus is truly going 'walkabout': 'Jesus went throughout Galilee, teaching in their synagogues and proclaiming the good news of the kingdom and curing every disease, and every sickness among the people. So his fame spread throughout all Syria, and they brought to him all the sick, those who were afflicted with various diseases and pains, demoniacs, epileptics, and paralytics, and he cured them. And great crowds followed him from Galilee, the Decapolis, Jerusalem, Judea, and from beyond the Jordan' (Matthew 4:23–25).

So we see the impact of Jesus' ministry not only spreading across the Jordan and up into Syria, but also right down to Jerusalem. This is not such an obscure area as we sometimes suppose, but a centre of trade, as we saw earlier. Communications seemed to run through Galilee and so the word spread.

Our host this week will be Abuna Elias Chacour and we shall also meet Palestinian peacemakers Mubarak Awad and Michail Fanous, and Jewish peacemakers Yehezkel and Dalia Landau.

Monday of week 4
Miracle at Capernaum

MARK 1:21–28

They went to Capernaum; and when the sabbath came, he entered the synagogue and taught. They were astounded at his teaching, for he taught them as one having authority, and not as the scribes. Just then there was in their synagogue a man with an unclean spirit, and he cried out, 'What have you to do with us, Jesus of Nazareth? Have you come to destroy us? I know who you are, the Holy One of God.' But Jesus rebuked him, saying, 'Be silent, and come out of him!' And the unclean spirit, convulsing him and crying with a loud voice, came out of him. They were all amazed, and they kept on asking one another, 'What is this? A new teaching—with authority! He commands even the unclean spirits, and they obey him.' At once his fame began to spread throughout the surrounding region of Galilee.

Mark portrays Jesus as an authoritative teacher, and this incident shows him as powerful both in deed and word. The service on the sabbath in the synagogue would have had prayers, readings from the scripture, and also teaching, and anyone of sufficient learning could be invited to teach. But the teaching of Jesus obviously amazed people. He was one who had authority 'and not as the scribes'. Their authority would have been appealing to scripture and to the words and deeds of other Jewish teachers. They would have been interpreters of the Law. Whereas, it seems that Jesus the teacher was confident in his own authority.

We also encounter Jesus the healer, as well as the teacher. A person comes who is psychologically disturbed and Jesus is able to show them his authority in action. Jesus is able—without any ritual or magical display—just by his words to sort out this disturbed person. 'Have you come to destroy us?' asks the evil spirit, and the answer is, of course, 'yes'. Jesus has come to destroy the grip of what holds people back and takes them in the wrong direction, thereby helping the person find their fulfilment and their 'life in all its fulness'.

Not surprisingly, his fame begins to spread, yet Jesus repeatedly asks people to keep quiet—he's not begging for a good PR person, he's not saying,

'Get a press release of this put out immediately—this will help to maximize my ministry.' Why? Jesus always chooses the path of humility and lets the deeds and the words speak for themselves. He won't use the spectacular to draw people any more than he would give in to that temptation when he was in the wilderness. I'm always nervous when people today advertise that they are miracle workers or healers because, although they would claim they do it in the name of Jesus, their method doesn't seem to be his method. It tends to accentuate the sense of the magical and when that happens it puts great power into the hands of the individual. Jesus rejected that power. He wasn't prepared to be followed as an instant problem-solver. He presented a much more holistic ministry. One of the temptations for preachers and healers is to be manipulative. Jesus resisted this—it immediately takes away the value of the very people to whom we are trying to proclaim this gospel of hope. To manipulate is to deny the power of God's Holy Spirit. It is the method of the doubter, not the method of the person who has the faith and the authoritative approach of Jesus.

So in Nazareth and in Capernaum we've seen Jesus starting to make this ministry tangible—not only by words but also by deeds—with the needy people that he meets day by day. This immediately has an application for us, as we think of the needy that we encounter day by day. The growth in the number of mentally ill people on the streets of our cities is a challenge for our mission. Kenneth Leech, in his book *We Preach Christ Crucified*, talks about the tremendous increase of homeless young people on the streets of Britain since his work started twenty-five years ago. And he says:

We have seen a massive increase, in both British and North American cities, in the numbers of young people forced on to the streets, more mentally ill people in the streets, more people dying, often literally of the cold. The change has been horrifying and yet what has been far worse has been the way in which so many of us have become acclimatised to the situation, inoculated against it. There has been a loss of passion, a loss of anger and of the impetus for change. The wounded Christ today is not crucified but ignored... At the same time there is no shortage of 'spirituality'. But we are being offered spirituality as another product on the market. Much of it lacks grief, struggle, rage and passion, those features which are... so central to the spirituality of the crucified God.

Thought

Is our Gospel 'privatized' or is it one that compels us into community with our brothers and sisters in Christ and then to reach out to the needy wherever we meet them in our communities?

The Sermon on the Mount

MATTHEW 5:1–3

When Jesus saw the crowds, he went up the mountain; and after he sat down, his disciples came to him. Then he began to speak, and taught them, saying: 'Blessed are the poor in spirit, for theirs is the kingdom of heaven.'

This passage follows the news that great crowds followed Jesus from all over Galilee, across the Jordan and even from down in Jerusalem, and now, when Jesus sees the crowd, he goes up a mountain and we get his most remarkable sermon. In Matthew, it is the start of Jesus' teaching.

Matthew puts it on a mountain (whereas Luke has the teaching 'on a level place'), and Matthew's reason is that a mountain is a place of revelation, like Sinai. Matthew wants us to see this on a par with the giving of the Ten Commandments. These are the commands of the new kingdom.

'Blessed are the poor' starts Luke in his beatitudes, and it looks as if Matthew added 'in spirit'. Maybe he wants to widen it out a bit whereas Luke has already shown us that Jesus sees himself as bringing good news to the poor. Wealth is not seen as evil, but there are warnings about it. It might take our mind off God, or indeed off the poor, and Luke goes on, after his beatitudes, to give his woes, and his first one is, 'But woe to you who are rich, for you have received your consolation.' In the teaching of the Sermon on the Mount, Jesus is showing us the priority values of God, and the first is care for the poor.

Jim Wallis, of the Sojourners community in Washington, has been a leading motivator in getting people to take seriously biblical Christianity's injunction to care for the poor and the needy. I find one of the illustrations of his that people remember best is the one of when he was at college and he and a friend decided to cut out of the Bible all the references to the poor. They ended up with this extraordinarily mutilated version, which they would hold up and say, 'this is the American Bible, full of holes'.

But it is also the Bible of so much Christianity. We take the bits we want and mould them in our own image, and so spirituality becomes personal and privatized. I quoted yesterday from Kenneth Leech, and he goes on to say, in his book, *We Preach Christ Crucified*:

Much contemporary spirituality lacks the imaginative encounter with poverty, pain and dereliction. It is a spirituality which has ceased to struggle and which therefore has ceased to be in Christ. So as our culture spawns numerous privatised spiritualities, thousands die of the cold. To recognise in the pain of others, in the broken and crushed people of the world, the form of the wounded Christ, is to recognise the strange and demanding nature of the Gospel call. It is the call to perform the corporal works of mercy: to feed the hungry; to clothe the naked; to shelter the homeless poor; to break the fetters of injustice; to give drink to the thirsty; to visit the sick; to bury the dead. It is a call to gird ourselves with Christ's dirty towel and to wash his feet, those bloody, wounded, exhausted feet. Christ's feet, his wounded hands and side, his broken heart, are not to be found only in ancient Jerusalem, but in Manchester and London, in Chicago and Boston, in Santiago and Johannesburg, in the back streets of the earth, wherever his sisters and brothers are crushed and broken and cast down as persons of no significance.

What can we say about Matthew's addition of 'in spirit'? Is there also a dimension here that should not be ignored? Some people are 'poor in spirit' because their spirits have been crushed and destroyed. They may not be economically poor, but they may have a terrible self-image. They may feel they are worthless, and this passage says that in the kingdom of God you are valuable. This passage could be taken in two ways. First, go and be a humble person who doesn't dominate others—have a simplicity of spirit rather than a swollen ego. At the same time, it can be taken to affirm those whose spirits have been crushed. Just as our spirits and personalities must be nurtured, so at the same time, it's not to be done at the expense of crushing other people.

Prayer

Lord, when our spirits are crushed and broken, remind us of our worth. Help us to see ourselves as treasured in the eyes of a loving God and then, Lord, remind us to be those who have a voluntary poverty of spirit so we do not impose ourselves on others, so we don't dominate or crush, or allow our ego to swell in a way that impinges on others. Instead may we reach out with your love, so others will know that they are cherished and valued by you. Show us the practical deeds to do today that will reflect your love. Amen.

The mournful and the meek

MATTHEW 5:4–5

'Blessed are those who mourn, for they will be comforted. Blessed are the meek, for they will inherit the earth.'

In some ways, today's first beatitude is a puzzle: why are those who mourn blessed? It seems to be a context that is very specific. It's those who mourn to see evil having its way on earth. How will these people be comforted? They will be comforted as they see the values of the community of God come into being, and as they are part of those who help those values to become real. In Luke it says, 'Blessed are you who weep now, for you will laugh.' The current pain and suffering and injustice gives cause for weeping but, as the kingdom of God is allowed to come in, there will be cause for laughter.

In Luke's Gospel, just before the Sermon on the Plain, Jesus had been up a mountain praying. Having spent the night in prayer, he calls his disciples and chooses twelve of them, and then he comes down and stands in a level place and he heals and he teaches. The Twelve are clearly seen to be symbolic of this new community, this new Israel—like leaders of the twelve tribes. Jesus then sets out the agenda of this new community that stretches beyond any national or geographical boundaries. This is the inclusive gospel, the inclusive kingdom. We are to be people who mourn over the imbalances and who mourn when we see the hurts and the suffering of our societies. If we were to be other than that—rejoicing in our personal salvation while ignoring the hurt around us—it would be a cruel faith. But to be those who mourn over what is wrong means that, in turn, as part of the community of this new kingdom, we will be working together to cause the circumstances that bring the laughter and the hope.

How many had mourned over the pain of apartheid in South Africa? I remember being told by some Christians to stop talking about the evil of apartheid in my concerts—I was being 'political'. They told me to look on the positive side of people coming to Christ and being healed in that country, and to ignore these 'political' statements. I wondered how they felt on the day Mandela was released, and on the inauguration of the new South Africa. Were they able to join in the laughter that was a witness to the whole world, or were they feeling fear and anxiety because they had not mourned at the injustice, and so perhaps they could not feel the joy when it was lifted? If we haven't mourned over what has happened in Rwanda or Bosnia or Chechnya or in the refugee camps of the West Bank, will we feel the comfort and the hope when these places rise again from the ashes of their destruction?

'Blessed are the meek, for they will inherit the earth.' Here Jesus quotes from Psalm 37:11, and the word 'meek' means 'slow to anger' or 'gentle with others'. Maybe one could even add 'gentle with God's creation'. Because, ironically, those who are gentle with God's creation may be the very ones who allow it to continue and, therefore, inherit it. At the moment, our greed and our dominance and our consumption of creation threatens its very existence. But blessed are those who are gentle and unselfish with it. Blessed are those who think of their neighbour, and those yet to come. Psalm 37 reminds us not to be envious of wrongdoers, for their days will be numbered; it reminds us to 'Trust in the Lord and do good; so you will live in the land and enjoy security.' It says, 'Refrain from anger, and forsake wrath' and then goes on to say, 'But the meek shall inherit the land, and delight themselves in abundant prosperity.' Why? Because they are the ones who will have walked in the just path and built a secure society; they will have seen injustice wither away as they refuse to accept it, because they commit themselves to the ways of God. These people will inherit the earth because they will have built a community where all can live together.

Prayer

We need your mother love O God to teach us to say yes
To all the ways of beauty, to all the ways that bless
To be gentle with creation and all God's creatures too
To treat the earth with kindness, to cherish and renew.

We need your mother love O God so we're numbered with the meek
Forgive our need to dominate over poor and weak.
And men over women and race over race
Forgive us for the fear that hides the human face.

We need your mother love O God to keep our spirits true
To the values of your Kingdom, to the attitudes from you.
Blessed are the merciful, blessed are the meek,
Blessed are the humble, blessed are the weak.

Garth Hewitt

The mountain of closeness

MATTHEW 5:6

'Blessed are those who hunger and thirst for righteousness, for they will be filled.'

The Sermon on the Mount is commemorated in a beautiful setting overlooking the Sea of Galilee from its northern shore. It is called the Mount of Beatitudes and there is a distinctive church built on the brow of the hill with a wonderful view across the lake. The church was built by Italian missionaries and the land was acquired by them in order to have a hospice here, to give pilgrims the opportunity to spend time in contemplation and prayer. Inside the church, the beatitudes are written in different languages around the wall. As I looked at the one in English, it struck me with added force, as it says, 'Blessed are those who hunger and thirst for *justice*, for they will be satisfied.'

On two occasions I have had the privilege of having Abuna Elias Chacour—a Greek Melkite priest from Galilee—come and expound the Sermon on the Mount to me on this spot. He is a remarkable peacemaker and I will tell you more of his story on Palm Sunday. Because of the strong teaching of his father about Jesus and the Sermon on the Mount, he has committed his life to the way of peace, and to introducing people to Jesus, the one he calls his 'Champion'. One of the things he reminded us of, as we sat on the Mount, was that this is a different mountain from the one where the Commandments were given. He says, 'Now compare that image with what happened on Mount Horeb in the Sinai, where no one was allowed even to touch the mountain. You needed to keep away, to keep afar. If you touched the mountain you were killed. Here, if you don't come closer, Jesus will call you. Please come closer, you poor, you paralysed, you sick man, you lady, come closer. I love you. I want to reveal to you one thing, that my Father loves you so much, that he trusts you also so much.'

So this is the mountain of closeness as opposed to the mountain that says keep far-off. This is the mountain of inclusiveness, as opposed to the mountain of exclusiveness. And then he goes on to say, 'Now when I tried to read what is written by St Matthew, I was bothered at the beginning. How can

I explain that to my Palestinian children?... I was born terrorized, like the children of Auschwitz, we were born terrorized because people had accepted to reduce the Jews to a vague entity, "dirty Jew", and that was the most barbaric thing to do to a human community. "Dirty Jew" and "Palestinian terrorist". We are not terrorists and they are not dirty, so what can I say to my children? "Happy are those who hunger and thirst for justice"? But they are not happy, they are starving, they are oppressed, they are in prison, they are living in the garbage place in Gaza, their bones are being broken, they are detained in prisons for six months, eight months, eighteen months, without any accusation. They are not happy, so I wonder how I can read that sermon... What if your hunger and your thirst are not for bread and for food, but for justice?... Please forget so many things you have learnt in church or outside the church, and try to be on this Mount of Beatitudes. As you see, it's no mount, it's the seaside and it's below sea-level. You are in the lowest place in the world.'

I wish you all could experience something of the passion of this remarkable peacemaker as he expounds, sitting on this mountain. This is not dry arid theology, this is theology that moved from the pain of Auschwitz and the pain of the Palestinian people, to apply the words of Jesus with an extraordinary relevance. His words, like the words of Jesus, have a poignancy. What do they mean, you wonder? What is the significance of being in the lowest place on earth? What is he saying? Perhaps something about humility. Perhaps something about the fact that we are all together at that point. Perhaps something about the fact we can fall no further, but we can find a path to help each other on the road upwards. Today's words remind us to be the ones who hunger and thirst for doing right, for seeing justice prevail. We will then be the ones who are satisfied when we see steps taken on the pathway to what is right and just. If we help to create a more caring, forgiving world, in return we will benefit from this. Again it's a reminder that those who grab to gain will ironically lose. It is in losing your life that you gain it. What an extraordinary gospel!

Prayer

God, our Father and our Mother, thank you that you say 'come closer' instead of 'stay far off'. Walk beside us on our journey and may we find satisfaction as we hunger for what is right and just. Amen.

Peacemakers

MATTHEW 5:9

'Blessed are the peacemakers, for they will be called children of God.'

When we were sitting with Elias Chacour on the Mount of Beatitudes he said, 'My compatriot, Jesus Christ, was in these places here, these very places. Don't forget to look around and to remember that it was from these hills, these waters, these trees that he got his inspiration. From these noises you may not pay attention to, these small insects, these small birds that sing the glory of God. You are worth much more than these birds. Listen to them.' Then he paused for us to listen to the noises around us. I'm someone who doesn't often do that, I'm busy, I'm active, I want to get to the nub of it. What's the heart of what you are saying, Elias? Let's get to it. Then he made me stop and listen to the sounds around me. And it was refreshing. I remember once at the Greenbelt Festival going in to hear Gerard Hughes and he was talking about a spirituality for those who are political activists and he made us stop and be silent and focus on the ground, on the grass, on the sights around us. As we sat there I was looking through a break in the tent at the beautiful countryside at Castle Ashby and I felt my soul being restored, just as it was by the Sea of Galilee. We need to take time to draw strength from the beauty and the refreshment of God's creation. Take time now to be silent, to forget about the things that are pushing in on you. Are there some noises of leaves in the trees or birds singing, or the sound of the wind? Maybe it would be good to take a walk outside and feel the refreshment of God's world as it ministers to you.

Abuna Elias then went on to talk to us about the way the Bible translates these words. He says that 'happy' is the worst translation. 'Blessed' he prefers, but he points out that the word he thinks Jesus used in the Aramaic was an active word, meaning 'go and do'. 'Go and create' these circumstances. In fact, he reads the beatitudes like this: 'Seeing the multitudes he went up onto a mountain and when he sat, his disciples came to him and he opened his mouth and taught them saying, "Get up, go ahead, move, do something. Yes, get your hands dirty, you poor in spirit, for yours is the kingdom of heaven. Get up, go ahead, do something, get your hands dirty you hungry and thirsty for justice. Get up, go ahead, don't contemplate but get your hands dirty if you want to be peacemakers, peacebuilders, peace constructors, and not peace contemplators. Do something about that." That makes sense to oppressed people and to oppressors as well.'

So Elias is reminding us to be people who go and do, to go and create these circumstances, to bring this kingdom into being, as we work together with Christ. Our contemplation is allowed but not if it stops there. We must go on to be doers. We need our moments of refreshment and silence, but we don't stay there, we're also to be doers of the word. It's the peacemakers who will be called the children of God because God is the peacemaker. He breaks down the divisions, he heals the wounds, he brings people to himself so that they can share with one another.

I remember in Lima in Peru seeing a wall that had been built on a place called Monterico, which means 'rich mountain' and the wall was built to keep the poor away from the rich. Christ comes to remove walls like this. In what ways are we divided—between rich and poor, between Jew and Gentile, between oppressed and oppressor, between male and female? We find that the divisions of nationality, race, religion and gender come down in Christ. Galatians 3:28 says, 'There is no longer Jew or Greek, there is no longer slave or free, there is no longer male and female; for all of you are one in Christ Jesus.'

In our society at the moment there's an increasing number of racial attacks. People are literally barricaded in their homes in fear in places such as the East End of London simply because they are Asian. People can't walk home safely at night like young Stephen Lawrence, who was murdered just because he was black. We are challenged by these things to root out the evil in our society, to break down that wall of division. We are to bring people of prejudice to the two-edged sword of the gospel, so that they can lose their fear and their hatred and find their home and openness in Christ.

Prayer

Lord, I want to be a child of God. Show me the path of peacemaking today. I bring my prejudices to you, and ask that you will continue to convert me day by day and step by step on the way, so that I never build up walls of division but become one of those that show that in Christ these divisions are finished. Amen.

Thought

Who brings about peace is called the companion of God in the work of creation.

Jewish saying

Breaking the spiral of violence

MATTHEW 5:38–45

'You have heard that it was said, "An eye for an eye and a tooth for a tooth." But I say to you, Do not resist an evildoer. But if anyone strikes you on the right cheek, turn the other also; and if anyone wants to sue you and take your coat, give your cloak as well; and if anyone forces you to go one mile, go also the second mile. Give to everyone who begs from you, and do not refuse anyone who wants to borrow from you.

'You have heard that it was said, "You shall love your neighbour and hate your enemy." But I say to you, Love your enemies and pray for those who persecute you, so that you may be children of your Father in heaven.'

The Sermon on the Mount is packed with teaching about the values of the kingdom of God and how we should live. But we need to go walking with Jesus again, so there will be just two more sections from the sermon: this one, on our need to love our enemies, and also Jesus' teaching on prayer.

Here Jesus starts off by quoting a legal rule from Exodus 21:23–25, 'you shall give life for life, eye for eye, tooth for tooth, hand for hand, foot for foot, burn for burn, wound for wound, stripe for stripe'. This was, in its context, a very humane passage. They were told don't take excessive revenge. If your eye is taken you're not to take a life. This in itself was a step forward within the Bible. We can trace the development of the theme of revenge and love of enemies. In Genesis 4:15 and 24, we find revenge being taken both sevenfold and seventy-sevenfold. So this then was a step forward—revenge should match what had happened. By the time we get to the book of Tobit in the Aprocrypha, it's moved forward yet again. In Tobit 4:15 we read, 'Do to no one what you would not want done to you.' This, of course, is put in a positive way by Jesus in the golden rule in the Sermon on the Mount, 'In everything do to others as you would have them do to you; for this is the law and the prophets.' But what Jesus was saying in our passage for today about loving our enemies takes it even further.

Today's passage is not an invitation for passive resignation, or indeed indifference, in the face of evil. In fact, this passage is what has underpinned the non-violent resistance of Mahatma Gandhi and Martin Luther King. Walter Wink has shown that in these passages there is more resistance of a non-violent sort than might originally be supposed. For instance, if someone takes your coat and you give your cloak, this is a reference to your undergarment. It leaves you naked and would have been very humiliating for the person who had done this. The goal of these actions is actually to shame your opponent. It's a policy for winning, not for passive resignation. Loving enemies and praying for those who persecute you is not some unobtainable idealism but a good plan for overcoming the opposition, and it has been used in campaigns, such as those of Gandhi and Martin Luther King, with great success. When Martin Luther King fell to his knees in the street with the others, in the days of the civil rights movements, and prayed, the world looked on appalled when the water cannons and the dogs were let loose on them. At that point Martin Luther King won. It was the same in South Africa, when Archbishop Desmond Tutu prayed for his persecutors and, indeed, pleaded with them to join him, those carrying the weapons were embarrassed and, again, in the eyes of the world, looked brutal and were losing the moral battle.

In pragmatic terms this passage has got some shrewd wisdom to teach. If we use violence in a cause, we have taken the moral low ground. This teaching of Jesus is extended in Romans 12:19–20, where, quoting from the Old Testament, Paul says, 'If your enemies are hungry, feed them; if they are thirsty, give them something to drink; for by doing this you will heap burning coals on their heads.' And then Paul adds, 'Do not be overcome by evil, but overcome evil with good.' Quoting here from Proverbs 25:21–22, he links in the words of Jesus in the Sermon on the Mount as a reminder that this is not a naive method. 'The burning coals on the head' is a reminder that this is a method that is effective, it's a method to lessen the cycle of violence and also to win against the aggressor. Our children are brought up on myths that violence succeeds, and then we wonder why our societies are violent. We need to teach them the strength of this alternative way. Violence does not bring solutions, it creates problems. The method of Jesus is a way to break the spiral of violence. If we use this method, what will we become? Truly 'children of our Father in heaven'.

Prayer

Lord, may we be generous spirited and strong in our resistance of evil, loving our enemies and praying for those who bring suffering in society. May we use the methods of Jesus to show the love of Jesus. Amen.

Journeying to peace with Mubarak Awad

Dedicated to non-violence

Mubarak Awad is committed to non-violence. We've already met his brother, Bishara, the President of Bethlehem Bible College. When they were young lads, in 1948, their father was killed. He was bringing someone who was injured—they don't know whether Jew or Arab—to their mother because she was a nurse. Mubarak saw the effect of his father's death on his mother, as she struggled to raise seven children, and her suffering affected him deeply. He feels issues of religion and race can be resolved without violence—people don't need to fight. We must look at our enemy as a human being.

The command of Jesus to 'love your enemy' underpins his commitment to non-violence. He says, 'Christ was telling us all to "love your enemy". As a Palestinian, I have to love the Israeli who is my enemy—to love an enemy is to disarm an enemy, and Christ is saying "disarm that enemy so you become equal".' Mubarak goes on to say that he has been very influenced by the Quakers and Mennonites (Mubarak's wife is a Quaker) who have opened his eyes to this route of pacifism. He says, 'Our life is too precious to kill for nationalism or for a flag.'

Mubarak is the Director of the Palestinian Centre for Non-Violence, and in his office in Jerusalem I noticed the works of Mahatma Gandhi. I asked him about Gandhi's influence. He said the influence was very important to him—this influence of non-violent action. 'Gandhi was pushing people to improve themselves and the philosophy of Gandhi is important because it leads you to practical non-violent action. For instance, to stand in front of an Israeli soldier and not to run.'

In 1988 the Israelis charged Mubarak with fourteen acts of non-violent activity and deported him. The United States intervened over his deportation so he was sent to New York. He is now allowed to come back for periods of up to three months but he hasn't been given his ID card back. As well as his Palestinian Centre for Non-Violence, he has also started the Palestinian Centre for Democracy in Elections. Mubarak says, 'We don't want to be like other Arab countries that don't have democracy.' Mubarak, motivated by the words of Jesus from the Sermon on the Mount, to love our neighbour, says we are to carry on doing this work and to empower ourselves with non-violent action and with truth.

Fourth Sunday
The parable of three trees and an open house

Dalia Ashkenazi was only eleven months old when she and her family arrived in Ramle, having emigrated to Israel, together with 50,000 other Jews from Bulgaria. Her family were settled in an empty Arab house and years later her father bought it from the State. Dalia grew up in that house, it was the only home she knew and she loved it—with its high ceilings, big windows and, most of all, the walled yard around it.

In the yard was a lemon tree which had been there when they arrived. It had plenty of fruit and they made lemonade from it. Also there was a jacaranda tree—her father planted this, and its leaves gave shade from the hot sun in summer. One day in July 1967, Dalia was home from university. The bell rang and three Palestinian men were at the gate. One was Bashir Al-Khayri—he said he had been born in the house and had been forced to leave at the age of six, and had not been allowed to see the house since. Now, with Israel occupying the West Bank, the Al-Khayri family could return to Ramle from Ramallah for the first time. Later Bashir's father, Ahmed Al-Khayri, came to visit the house he had built in the 1930s. He was old and blind and he caressed the stone walls of the house. He asked if the lemon tree he had planted was still in the back yard. Under the tree, tears rolled down his cheeks and when he left Dalia gave him a cluster of lemons to take back to Ramallah. On nights when he couldn't sleep, he would pace to and fro holding one of these lemons.

The years went by and Dalia's parents died. She inherited the house, and she married American Jewish immigrant Yehezkel Landau. Yehezkel and Dalia sought out Bashir and began to talk about the future of the house—they wanted to share it. Bashir was very moved, and he suggested the house should serve the needs of the local Palestinian population in Ramle, particularly early childhood education. The Landaus were delighted with this and, in addition, wanted it to be a place where Jew and Palestinian could meet. So on 27 April 1991 Open House was launched as a centre for the development of the Arab child and as a centre for Jewish-Palestinian co-existence with all sorts of activities.

The Al-Khayri family is Muslim, the Landaus are Jewish, and the third

Christian corner of the 'Abrahamic triangle' came into the picture through the appointment of the Christian Michail Fanous as the Director of Open House. His family has been in Ramle for 700 years and his brother Samwil is the local Anglican priest. Michail not only works at Open House but also serves on the Ramle city council. He says about Open House, 'I feel that this house is a small story, but it tells the story of all of Israel and Palestine. In 1948 most of the Arabs of Ramle had to leave. The same year Jewish families came to Ramle and the rest of Israel. So when Dalia came here and told me she feels this house belongs to her and to the Al-Khayri family, for me it was a sign of reconciliation between Israel and Palestine.'

In mid-January 1995 comes the story of the third tree. In the Jewish calendar it was the New Year of the trees (Tu B'shvat) and it was Arbor day for the Arabs of Palestine and Jordan. So Open House held a moving ceremony planting a young olive tree. Two of Bashir's sisters, Nuha from Ramallah and Chanoum from Amman in Jordan, came to join the Landaus and Michail Fanous to plant an olive tree in the yard. Yehezkel and Dalia's six-and-a-half-year-old son Raphael was with them—they didn't send him to school that day, so he could help dig the hole and plant the tree. And the Arab children from the kindergarten were present. They planted the tree as a symbol of their common attachment to the land and to ecology and dedicated it to heal the wounds of the land. They prayed for the fruit of justice and peace which 'all the children of Abraham in this Holy Land long to taste'. Their prayer was that just as the lemon tree had made lemonade for two families, so the olives and olive oil from this tree, when it is grown, should bless the peoples of this land.

There is also a parable within a parable because when Dalia's father planted the jacaranda tree, he decided after he'd planted it that he didn't want it and he chopped it down but, fortunately, he didn't uproot it and it grew back in the form that it has now with many big branches off the trunk. For Yehezkel and Dalia it symbolizes a number of things, resurrection or the life force overcoming our destructive tendencies, wilful or otherwise, towards the creation, and it also symbolizes for them plurality on a common base such as in the Abrahamic family. Yehezkel says, 'We have a common father, Abraham, and a common mother, Jerusalem, and a common parent in heaven and on earth, and we can all be siblings in the family of God with different identities, and that's what this tree symbolizes for me.' And Yehezkel sees the Open House project, like Michail, as a microcosm of the whole Holy Land, which he sees as God's laboratory and a microcosm of the whole of the creation. Three families of the three faiths, Abrahamic siblings, trying to share the Abrahamic blessing, to plant seeds and bear fruit for everybody, to share the fruits of this abundant creation. Together they've been slowly building this project, as a centre of co-existence and mutual understanding and respect. From Open House they want that to spread out to Ramle, and from Ramle, ideally, to all of Israel/Palestine.

Prayer

Lord, we thank you for the symbol of the jacaranda tree, a sign of resurrection overcoming the destructive, and we pray that this hope will be reflected in Open House, then in the community of Ramle, and throughout the land of Israel/Palestine. Amen.

Journeying to peace with
Yehezkel Landau

Peace movements and biblical faith

Yehezkel Landau feels that peace movements everywhere fail because they only do the prophetic work of criticizing injustice, they don't do enough of the priestly work of transforming hearts by mediating forgiveness through sacrifice. He adds, 'That's what I think priests in both Jewish and Christian traditions are called to do, that's their vocation to mediate God's love and forgiveness through sacrifice.' Yehezkel goes on to talk of 'sacrificing something on the material plane, to get a spiritual blessing and healing in return. Whether it's the body and blood of Christ or whether it's animal bodies—there's some ancient wisdom that we have lost as Jews and Christians. My understanding of Israel and Palestine is that both peoples have to suffer an amputation, a part of their physical body, so that the state of Israel will be smaller than the land of Israel, and the state of Palestine will be smaller than the land of Palestine. Parts will have to be sacrificed for the common blessing and for the common act of consecration or sanctifying the land which is holy together. This microcosm,' he says, referring to Open House, 'this house, has been sacrificed by one family against its will and sacrificed by the other family wilfully, and it is now a sacrificial offering to the creator and to creation and, with God's blessing, it will serve the purpose that is underneath the whole creation and why we are here to begin with.'

I asked Yehezkel for a verse that underpins his motivation and he quoted from Zechariah 8:16, 'These are the things which you shall do—speak everyone the truth to his fellows; truth and justice-with-peace shall you administer in your gates.' For Yehezkel this underpins his commitment to peace and he says, 'Now that the peace negotiations have begun between Israelis and Palestinians, the diplomacy would stand a better chance of success, in my judgement, if the moral and spiritual truths of the biblical faith and tradition were heeded. In particular, if we take Zechariah's words as reflecting what is required for a society free of conflict then we might paraphrase his teaching in this way: We suffer violence because we do not rectify injustices, and those injustices persist as long as we fail to speak truth to one another.'

Week Five
Northern Galilee

W e've had a week sitting by the Sea of Galilee, a beautiful and inspirational setting and yet very challenging and motivating. But now it's time to start walking again with Jesus. We've seen the new command-ments of his kingdom and now we'll walk around with him in the Galilee area, and even up as far as the

borders of Syria to Caesarea Philippi. Before going up to Caesarea Philippi we'll have our final session from the Sermon on the Mount. In the midst of this practical teaching on how to live, how to care for others and how to give, comes how to pray.

Then we'll move away from Galilee and head up to the northern tip of modern Israel. I wonder what image you have of the weather conditions surrounding Jesus as he walked around in Palestine in those days. Before I went to the Holy Land, I think I felt that it was always vaguely warm and, presumably, always pretty mild apart from the occasional storm on the Sea of Galilee! But I have shivered in Galilee in winter-time and Caesarea Philippi I saw in the coldest of conditions. The drive up to Caesarea Philippi is through a part of Israel which has many of the new immigrants from Eastern Europe and has quite a separate feel to other parts of Israel. It's strange how architecture can dictate feeling. When I'm in West Jerusalem, I feel I'm in Western Europe, in some parts of Israel it could be Switzerland or Austria. But as one heads up into the northern part of Israel it seems like being in Poland or another part of Eastern Europe. This area is only a short distance from the remains of the city of Dan, and the Old Testament describes the length of the land as from Dan to Beersheba, so even then it was the northern tip.

When we came here it was a cold winter's evening. There was snow on Mount Hermon, so we decided to drive up to the snow line and there was a barrier across the road. We were given permission to go on higher to take photos. As we did, we passed a group of young Israeli soldiers who were on some training march. They surrounded our vehicle, joking and pleading for a lift. They looked ill-equipped, surprisingly so, but an officer came and dismissed them and we drove on up. Another couple of soldiers waved at us further up, asking for us to stop. We assumed they were pretending they were also in need of help, and joking as the previous group, and we drove on. We got up to the snow line, which looked dramatic and beautiful and we looked towards Syria. The road, however, was treacherous, and we decided not to continue. We turned our vehicle round and came down, only to find that one of the young soldiers who had waved to us was lying on the ground and the other one was desperately trying to stop us. The young lad was in a terrible state of hypothermia and, as I helped to carry him into the vehicle, I was shocked at how soaked through and cold he was. The other soldier had a radio with him and help was obviously on the way, because we hadn't gone too far before another vehicle had come alongside us to take the lad. My image of Palestine in Jesus' time was far from images of snow and bad conditions, and we easily sanitize the whole setting of the Gospels.

The Archbishop of Canterbury, George Carey, has warned that the Holy Land will turn into a 'Disney World' for Christians from around the world to visit; but there will be no Christians left in it to welcome them soon. He was commenting on the very difficult struggle for the indigenous Christian church, which is largely a Palestinian church. But also I think his point is applicable to our view of the Holy Land. We can make it a sort of Disney World where Jesus pops up looking like someone out of a Hollywood epic and where the weather conditions are subject more to the director's whims. The cold on Mount Hermon and shivering in Galilee have been good for my understanding of the flesh-and-blood Jesus who walked here.

This week we will meet two Jewish women who are peacemakers: one a Christian and a lawyer—Lynda Brayer; and the other a journalist and an activist—Roni Ben Efrat. Also on Sunday we'll meet Palestinian Christian Shehadeh Shehadeh in Haifa.

How to pray

MATTHEW 6:7–15

'When you are praying, do not heap up empty phrases as the Gentiles do; for they think that they will be heard because of their many words. Do not be like them, for your Father knows what you need before you ask him.

'Pray then in this way:
Our Father in heaven,
hallowed be your name.
Your kingdom come.
Your will be done,
on earth as it is in heaven.
Give us this day our daily bread.
And forgive us our debts,
as we also have forgiven our debtors.
And do not bring us to the time of trial,
but rescue us from the evil one.

'For if you forgive others their trespasses, your heavenly Father will also forgive you; but if you do not forgive others, neither will your Father forgive your trespasses.'

Just before our passage for today, Jesus teaches that when we pray, we shouldn't be like the hypocrites, doing it in public to be seen by others, but instead we should go into our room and shut the door and pray to our Father who sees in secret. Obviously there is communal prayer, Jesus himself went to the synagogues and prayed—and it is essential that we are part of the community of prayer. But also we need to find time alone with God.

Lynda Brayer is a Jewish Catholic lawyer who lives in Jerusalem. She particularly defends the rights of Palestinians as well as Jewish people, and is committed to justice for all. She works for the Society of St Yves, a legal resource centre for human rights. It is a taxing and difficult job, and when I asked her how she managed it, she pointed out that twice a day she goes to church to draw her strength from God. The more we are committed to living for God, the more we need to take those moments of stillness where we allow ourselves to be refreshed by God. Sometimes just to be still, and to say nothing, and other times to talk things over in the presence of God.

So what practical advice does Jesus give? First of all, there's no need to heap up the empty phrases—it's not the quantity of words that impresses God. Sometimes I hear people talking about prayer meetings almost in a superstitious way. Something hasn't worked well because we haven't done enough prayer, and prayer in itself becomes a busy, busy activity. But here Jesus gives us some clues. Take time to pray, but don't heap up the empty phrases. We are not heard for the many words. After all, our Father knows what we need before we even ask.

It was the custom of a religious community to have its own distinctive prayer, and this one is very significant for the new community of Jesus. It starts off reminding them of this loving, caring parent and then it's a prayer that the values of this compassionate God will come into being. It ends with forgiveness, the attitude that we need to have in order to be the people of this community, just as God, as a loving parent, forgives us. If we forgive others we will be forgiven, but if we don't forgive others, neither will our Father forgive us our trespasses. We can't deal with God in one compartment of our lives and with our fellow humans in another. What is required is this relationship of mutual forgiveness. Indeed, the Sermon on the Mount ends with a reminder to be doers of the word, 'Everyone who hears these words of mine and acts on them will be like a wise man who built his house on the rock.'

Just before that Jesus has given a severe warning that, 'Not everyone who says to me, "Lord, Lord," will enter the kingdom of heaven, but only the one who does the will of my Father in heaven. On that day many will say to me, "Lord, Lord, did we not prophesy in your name, and cast out demons in your name, and do many deeds of power in your name?" Then I will declare to them, "I never knew you; go away from me, you evildoers"' (Matthew 7:21–23). So it's not enough to do acts of power in Jesus' name, or even cast out demons and prophesy. We must do the will of his Father. So we need to keep on praying, 'Your kingdom come. Your will be done' and to pray that it will be done through us.

Prayer

Our Father in heaven,
hallowed be your name.
Your kingdom come.
Your will be done,
on earth as it is in heaven.
Give us this day our daily bread.

And forgive us our debts,
as we also have forgiven our debtors.
And do not bring us to the time of trial,
but rescue us from the evil one.
Amen.

Thought

I asked Lynda Brayer what was her motivation in her work
for peace.

'I would say that the guiding biblical principle for me is what
Jesus said, "I am the way, and the truth, and the life." I say this
particularly as a lawyer because without the concept of truth we do
not have an understanding of reality and therefore we can never
come to full life. For me that is the ultimate guide and I can hang on
because I know that there is another truth, and if I hang on maybe
we will come to some better life.'

Lynda Brayer (Jewish Christian lawyer for human rights)

Tuesday of week 5
Caesarea Philippi

MATTHEW 16:13–20

Now when Jesus came into the district of Caesarea Philippi, he asked his disciples, 'Who do people say that the Son of Man is?' And they said, 'Some say John the Baptist, but others Elijah, and still others Jeremiah or one of the prophets.' He said to them, 'But who do you say that I am?' Simon Peter answered, 'You are the Messiah, the Son of the living God.' And Jesus answered him, 'Blessed are you, Simon son of Jonah! For flesh and blood has not revealed this to you, but my Father in heaven. And I tell you, you are Peter, and on this rock I will build my church...' Then he sternly ordered the disciples not to tell anyone that he was the Messiah.

The area of Caesarea Philippi is now called Banias, which is an adaptation of the earlier name Panias, which was a city here in the first century BC dedicated to the god Pan. Augustus gave the city to Herod the Great, who built an elaborate palace in his honour, and after Herod's death his younger son Philip, who became Tetrarch of Galilee, renamed the city Caesarea Philippi to distinguish it from Caesarea Maritime on the coast. Later there was a Christian community here, which suffered persecution from its predominantly pagan neighbours. It's in the southern foothills of Mount Hermon and the site of Banias is owned by the Israeli authorities and is preserved as a nature park. Perhaps as Jesus and his disciples were walking around, they noticed some of the niches which would have contained statues to the god Pan, and I can imagine them chatting about this and discussing what people said about the ancient Greek god Pan who was reputed to protect flocks and herds. Then Jesus asked the question, 'Who do people say that the Son of Man is?'

It's interesting to hear what the disciples reply. In all of their comments they see a prophetic figure—then Jesus asks them who they think he is, and Peter responds, 'You are the Messiah' or 'You are the Christ.' What does this word 'Christ' mean? It has come to be almost Jesus' surname but, in fact, it meant the 'anointed one' and during the period in between the Old and the New Testament there developed a concept of '*the* anointed one', to whom the

Jewish people were looking forward. Jesus is being identified with this person in this reference by Peter. 'Anointed' in what sense? Kings, priests or prophets were all anointed with oil for the tasks they had to do, so maybe in this description we can see aspects of all three of these roles in Jesus. The concept of the Christ or the Messiah was not too tightly defined, so we find that the Qumran community, of whom we know much because of the discovery of the Dead Sea Scrolls, seems to have anticipated two Messiahs, one royal and one priestly. Jesus is obviously concerned that, because there are so many interpretations of what Messiah or Christ may mean, he will be misinterpreted so the disciples are not to tell anyone that he has this role, for he will be defining the word as he goes along.

Immediately he then starts to talk about the fact that he must go to Jerusalem to suffer and die. And these very events, as well as Jesus's teaching, start to define and, indeed, revolutionize, the way the word Messiah was understood. David Brown, in his book *The Word To Set You Free* (SPCK), talking of this title of Messiah/Christ, says, 'So only slowly does Jesus accept this title of himself, as he tries first to reeducate his disciples as to what being God's anointed might involve.' Earlier he has been talking about the word Jesus and Joshua having a common root and that Matthew sees this as significant, and that the name means 'God saves':

> *Instead of the Old Testament Joshua who did not hesitate even to use genocide as part of his programme for the liberation of the land here we have the New Testament Jesus excluding no-one, but instead extending his loving care to all, including even the hated occupying power, the Romans, and the despised neighbour, the Samaritans. Again, instead of the Empire of David and Solomon which included most of present-day Jordan, Syria and Lebanon, his messianic kingdom was to be a kingdom without frontiers, the kingdom reclaimed on a cross, as the penitent thief so clearly recognised: 'remember me when you come into your kingdom' (Luke 23:42). Again, instead of a resplendent and purified temple, this priestly Messiah inaugurated a temple of his body: 'destroy this temple and I shall rebuild it in three days.' In other words, the priest was also the sacrificial victim, the one who brought new life to us all not through an exclusivest cult, but by dying in order that we might live, by opening the way of love to all.*

Thought

Who do people say Jesus is today? Or is it even a question that impinges on many people? Spend some time thinking about your idea of Jesus. Have you thought of him more as an exclusive Old Testament figure, or more like the picture that David Brown gives of the New Testament Jesus excluding no one? Pause to think about the one who sends his love to all.

Wednesday of week 5
He must go to Jerusalem

MATTHEW 16:21-28

From that time on, Jesus began to show his disciples that he must go to Jerusalem and undergo great suffering at the hands of the elders and chief priests and scribes, and be killed, and on the third day be raised. And Peter took him aside and began to rebuke him, saying, 'God forbid it, Lord! This must never happen to you.' But he turned and said to Peter, 'Get behind me, Satan! You are a stumbling block to me; for you are setting your mind not on divine things but on human things.'

Then Jesus told his disciples, 'If any want to become my followers, let them deny themselves and take up their cross and follow me. For those who want to save their life will lose it, and those who lose their life for my sake will find it. For what will it profit them if they gain the whole world but forfeit their life? Or what will they give in return for their life? For the Son of Man is to come with his angels in the glory of his Father, and then he will repay everyone for what has been done. Truly I tell you, there are some standing here who will not taste death before they see the Son of Man coming in his kingdom.'

In yesterday's passage Peter stated that Jesus is the Christ, the Son of the living God, and Jesus affirmed him with tremendous words, using a pun as he did so, calling him Peter the Rock and, no doubt, standing by the rock face of Caesarea Philippi as the water gushes out, he would have pointed to one of the rocks as he said this. Today's passage follows on directly and we get the impression that Jesus and the disciples are still wandering around amongst the villages or in the district of Caesarea Philippi.

Having had the discussion that he is the Messiah, he then starts to tell them that he must go to Jerusalem and suffer and be killed and rise again. This is the role for the 'anointed' one. He has been anointed in order to go to his throne, which is a cross. In this role, he will be redefining the word 'king' as well as being both priest and victim. And Peter, who has just been so delighted with his discovery that Jesus is the Christ, cannot cope with this interpretation of the Messiah. To suffer and die is not the image that he has for the anointed one, and he is appalled. Jesus turns on him forcefully, because Peter is offering him the worldly view—the worldly way. To suffer and die is not the world's way to achieve things and Peter is playing the role of the tempter that we met in the wilderness in the first week. He wants another way, an easier route. He wants a route maybe of glory, but not a route via the cross. So Jesus rejects the temptation of Peter and goes on to tell the Twelve that they must take up the cross, deny themselves, and follow him if they want to be his disciples. He points out it is a route of self-denial, a route of losing their lives but, ironically, in so doing, they will find life. This saying expresses a deep psychological truth, that happiness somehow eludes those who seek it directly instead of, first of all, seeking the will of God and doing what is right.

Jesus then talks of coming in judgment to repay everyone for what has been done. And this section will be extended in Matthew 25, which starts off in almost the same way:

> 'When the Son of Man comes in his glory, and all the angels with him... he will... separate... the sheep and the goats, and he will put the sheep at his right hand and the goats at the left. Then the king will say to those at his right hand, "Come you that are blessed by my Father, inherit the knigdom prepared for you from the foundation of the world; for I was hungry and you gave me food, I was thirsty and you gave me something to drink, I was a stranger and you welcomed me, I was naked and you gave me clothing, I was sick and you took care of me, I was in prison and you visited me."'

Then the familiar discussion takes place with the people saying, '"Lord, when was it that we saw you [like this]?" And the king will answer them, "Truly, I tell you, just as you did it to the least of these who are members of my family, you did it to me."'

Then today's passage ends with the odd words that 'there are some standing here who will not taste death until they see the Son of Man coming in his kingdom'. If it's the fulness of the kingdom of God that is being referred to here, as at the end of time, then obviously Jesus got it wrong. But it seems more likely, since the transfiguration immediately follows this passage, that it's a reference to what is about to happen... in tomorrow's passage.

Prayer

Under the gaze of that elusive God, master of wild beauty and of sudden fear, where streams of living water are no metaphor, but rushing past your feet, you ask the question. Who am I? Whom can I trust and work with? What will be the cost? O God, just as the Jordan leaps here to life and runs, so give your tired people energy to turn again, to think fresh thoughts and risk a new direction. Amen.

Janet Morley, written at Caesarea Philippi,
in *Companions of God*, Christian Aid

Thursday of week 5
A baptism of glory

Six days later, Jesus took with him Peter and James and his brother John and led them up a high mountain, by themselves. And he was transfigured before them, and his face shone like the sun, and his clothes became dazzling white. Suddenly there appeared to them Moses and Elijah, talking with him. Then Peter said to Jesus, 'Lord, it is good for us to be here; if you wish, I will make three dwellings here, one for you, one for Moses, and one for Elijah.' While he was still speaking, suddenly a bright cloud overshadowed them, and from the cloud a voice said, 'This is my Son, the Beloved; with him I am well pleased; listen to him!'

No one knows for sure which is the mountain of transfiguration and traditionally Mount Tabor, just east of Nazareth in Galilee, has been the site and several churches have been built on it. But modern scholars now feel the much higher Mount Hermon is a more likely location, and in terms of proximity in the text it would seem to make sense. So without making any strong claims for it, we will place the transfiguration here, rather than Mount Tabor or even Mount Carmel. It could be, therefore, that for this story we are right up in what is now called the Golan Heights on the snow-capped Jabal al-Sheikh or Mount Hermon. Jabal al-Sheikh means 'the mountain of the old man'. Mount Hermon is a symbolic spot, a mixture of international borders and military 'no go' areas. It's one of the places in the country where the conflict of the Middle East becomes painfully visible. Within the shadow of Mount Hermon lie four Druze villages, which are separated from their families in Syria by a fence, where they go and shout to one another and thereby keep in touch with their relatives and friends in Syria—this area was Syria until 1967.

The passage starts off with the phrase 'after six days' and probably this is not a literal period of time but symbolic, because in Exodus 24:13–16 there is the story of Moses going up with Joshua and Aaron and Hur up Mount Sinai. When Moses goes up the mountain a cloud covers it. The cloud symbolizes the glory of the Lord and covers the mountain for six days, and on the seventh day God called to Moses out of the cloud. 'Now the appearance of the glory of the Lord was like a devouring fire on the top of the mountain in the sight of the people of Israel.' Obviously there is a parallel here and a sense in which they have already gone through the six days so now the glory of the Lord will be revealed. It also seems to be that 'after six days' seems to suggest that this could be the last day of the festival of booths or tabernacles. In Deuteronomy 16:13–15 it says, 'You shall keep the festival of booths for seven days.' And, again, this may be a suggestion that this is the last day of that festival—which is why Peter asks for three booths to be built. Anyway, the three disciples, Peter, James and John, who will reappear with Jesus in the Garden of Gethsemane, are with him up this high mountain.

The idea of transfiguration was common in classical paganism and Luke feels it is best to avoid the term altogether. Something happened to Jesus and he becomes in some way changed and he shines brightly symbolizing the glory of God upon him. At this point he is joined by Moses and Elijah—Moses, who represents the Law of the Old Testament and Elijah who represents the Prophets. This is a turning point of Jesus' ministry. He has just spoken of going towards his death and this incident shows that the road that Jesus is pursuing is in accordance with the Law and the Prophets. In Luke, he actually mentions what they were talking about, 'They appeared in glory and were speaking of his departure, which he was about to accomplish at Jerusalem.' It is almost a baptism moment. Just as the baptism of Jesus by John started his ministry and a voice speaks from heaven and says very much what is said here, 'You are my Son, the Beloved; with you I am well pleased.' This time there is the additional command to 'listen to him'. This baptism of glory prepares the way for the journey to the cross. Just like the baptism passage, there is a quote from Psalm 2:7 and a link in with Deuteronomy 18:15, and Matthew has added a reference to Isaiah 42:1 and in all of these passages what is being suggested is that Jesus is Son of God, suffering servant, and a prophet like Moses.

Thought

Peter wanted to prolong the experience and hold on to it by building three tabernacles and, in some ways, this has happened on Mount Tabor, with the building of churches on the top. But we are not to fossilize our experiences, but rather use them as the motivation on our journey. From the mountain-top experience, the disciples were plunged down into the valley and then onward, as Jesus set his face towards Jerusalem. We are not to keep trying to repeat our most moving moments, but to use them to motivate us to walk in the footsteps of Jesus. Too often we are trying to clamber back up the mountain, whilst God is telling us, 'Walk in the valley with compassion, get those fences down which divide people, bring them together in community, and chase away the destructive demons.'

A meal that satisfies

JOHN 6:5–11

When [Jesus] looked up and saw a large crowd coming toward him, Jesus said to Philip, 'Where are we to buy bread for these people to eat?'... Philip answered him, 'Six months' wages would not buy enough bread for each of them to get a little.' One of his disciples, Andrew, Simon Peter's brother, said to him, 'There is a boy here who has five barley loaves and two fish. But what are they among so many people?' Jesus said, 'Make the people sit down.' Now there was a great deal of grass in the place; so they sat down, about five thousand in all. Then Jesus took the loaves, and when he had given thanks, he distributed them to those who were seated; so also the fish, as much as they wanted.

Today we are back by the Sea of Galilee and if we follow the traditional tourist site of the 'feeding of the five thousand' we are at Tabgha, which is situated at the top of the Sea of Galilee, not far from Capernaum. Since the fourth century this has been the traditional site for the 'feeding of the five thousand'. A church was built over what was said to be the original spot in the fourth century and another church was erected over it in the fifth century. There are some fine mosaics here which date from that time. The only problem is that the Gospels actually locate the story of the 'feeding of the five thousand' on the east side of Galilee, but because that was difficult for access, it was decided to put the site this side for the sake of pilgrims! But it provides a convenient place for thinking about the miracle. I find that getting away from traditional sites is the moment when you feel closest to the land where Jesus walked, and to be in a place where someone hasn't built a church can be a relief!

In this incident we have both a miracle and an acted parable. It's a very human story with Philip looking alarmed and pointing out that six months' wages would not get enough bread for all these people. Andrew then brings the boy with the five loaves and two fish. In some ways it's strange he even mentions it, and he adds, 'But what are they among so many people?' Jesus then organizes the sitting of people in groups. Then we discover an almost eucharistic pattern as Jesus takes the bread and, when he has given thanks, he distributes it to those who are seated. All the Gospels have this story, and two—Matthew and Mark—also contain a feeding of 4,000. Likewise, they all include the blessing of the bread, breaking it, and then sharing. It seems that this is a forerunner of the communion meal. Not only are the people satisfied, but there are twelve baskets left—a symbolic number to suggest the twelve tribes under the twelve disciples. This symbolizes the new Israel, the new community, which Jesus feeds and satisfies as the bread of life. In John this miracle is used as a prelude to Jesus talking about being the bread of life, 'I am the bread of life. Whoever comes to me will never be hungry... Your ancestors ate the manna in the wilderness, and they died. This is the bread that comes down from heaven, so that one may eat of it and not die... Whoever eats of this bread will live forever; and the bread that I will give for the life of the world is my flesh' (John 6:35–51).

So this remarkable story, that is so important that it is in all the Gospels, looks back to the Old Testament with the manna coming for the children of Israel. The three Synoptic Gospels even mention that it was in a desert place—maybe there is a hint of wilderness. Then this miracle also looks forward to the new community of the kingdom of God, who draw their strength and are fully satisfied as they feed on Jesus Christ, the bread of life and the true vine.

Thought

Imagine yourself as the little lad. Sensibly you have brought some food and now you are being pushed to the front of this huge crowd, and it seems ridiculous. What, indeed, is this amongst so many people? Think of yourself, with your talents and your abilities and your gifts, and imagine those as five loaves and two fish. How often I've heard people say, 'But I have no gifts or no talents' or 'What can I do to help a situation? I can do nothing.' This story reminds us to bring whatever we have to Jesus, however small it may look, however hopeless, and not to underestimate the impact of Jesus blessing it and using it in the service of his kingdom.

Thought

*Remember the lad who gave what he had
For Jesus to use so the hungry were fed?
If we play our part with what we can give
For Jesus to use—then others will live.*

Five loaves and two small fish—
Five loaves and two small fish—
It may not look a lot on the dish—
But when Jesus said the grace, they all had full plates.

Garth Hewitt

Prayer

Father, you have given us Jesus Christ, who is the true bread from heaven. He is the manna of the New Covenant which came down from heaven and gives life to the world. Jesus said, 'I am the bread of life; he who comes to me will not hunger, and he who believes in me will never thirst.' Father deepen my faith in Christ so he may fill me with eternal life and raise me up on the last day. Feed me with Christ's own body and blood, for unless I eat his flesh and drink his blood I will not have life in me... Father, I thank you for inviting me to eat at your table, so enabling me to taste for myself that the Lord is very sweet.

From Peter De Rosa, A Bible Prayer Book for Today

Father and son reunion

L U K E 1 5 : 1 1 – 2 4

Then Jesus said, 'There was a man who had two sons. The younger of them said to his father, "Father, give me the share of the property that will belong to me." So he divided his property between them. A few days later the younger son gathered all he had and travelled to a distant country, and there he squandered his property in dissolute living. When he had spent everything, a severe famine took place throughout the country, and he began to be in need... So he set off and went to his father. But while he was still far off, his father saw him and was filled with compassion; he ran and put his arms around him and kissed him. Then the son said to him, "Father, I have sinned against heaven and before you; I am no longer worthy to be called your son." But the father said, "... let us eat and celebrate; for this son of mine was dead and is alive again; he was lost and is found!"'

We won't have long to dwell on the parables of Jesus as we walk around the Holy Land, but one of the things we need to remember is Jesus was a superb storyteller. This story has some unique features about it. There are two sons, and one of them asks for something absolutely unheard of in Middle Eastern culture. It was unheard of for a father to share out the inheritance whilst he is still alive, and the younger brother's request is, in fact, a wish for his father's death. The request, therefore, is seen as a profound breakdown of relationship between the father and the son. The father's response is unusual as well in Middle Eastern custom. The father would be expected to explode at such a request and to try and discipline the son. So Jesus' listeners would have been shocked. Also, as the story goes on and the son spends the inheritance amongst Gentiles, they would again be shocked, as this would be considered to go against the customs of the extended family in the local community. So there's breakdown of relationship not only between the father and the son but also with the community at large.

The elder son also, in verse 12, seems to receive his share of the inheritance. Instead of protesting loudly and refusing to take it, he just keeps quiet and accepts it. This again suggests that his relationship with his father is not good. Kenneth Bailey, in his book *Poet and Peasant* points out that in Middle Eastern customs, when relationships have broken down, a third party is selected to act as reconciler. In this case, the elder son should have played this role because of the closeness of his relationship.

Peacemaking is restoring right relationships, making things whole. Sometimes people feel that peacemaking is somehow stopping conflict. That is part of it, but it is actually the restoring of right relationships that is the real role of the peacemaker, and the elder son is refusing to play that part.

So now the younger son goes off to a far country, wastes his money and then experiences famine. So here is this lonely Jew in a far country without money or friends in a time of famine and in his desperation he accepts the job of feeding the pigs. Now what happens?—'He came to himself.' So he heads back, and then an extraordinary thing happens. It is undignified for an older person to run in Eastern custom—the more significant you are, the slower you walk. But the boy is about to face the wrath of the village community to whom he is returning and Kenneth Bailey says, 'The father then runs this gauntlet for him, assuming a humiliating posture in the process!' And so, on the edge of the village, there is the reconciliation, and it is at this point that the son repents, because his father has come running to him, has done this humble act to save his son from suffering further indignity. So the father's acts have been so significant that he doesn't have to speak. He has run because of his compassion and he has put his arms around his son and he has kissed him. It is a public acceptance seen by all.

We can almost hear the crowd 'oohing and aahing' as Jesus tells this story. It is an amazing story of God's grace reaching out to us, even when we have, so to speak, slapped him in the face and rejected him. No matter how much we insult the Father, or reject him, or cause the relationship to be broken down, he is prepared to show humble love and come running towards us, to restore and to heal that broken relationship.

If we had had our dignity wounded in this way, we would no doubt stand on our rights and demand an apology before accepting the son back. This parable tells us something about the nature of God, that he does not stand on wounded dignity like that. It reminds us in the area of peacemaking that there must be steps taken that go to meet the other person. To stand still at the place where we were wounded, or even to retreat backwards, does not give hope. Peacemakers are those who walk forward, often at great cost to themselves of looking foolish. Gordon Wilson, whose daughter was killed in the Enniskillen bomb in Northern Ireland, talked of forgiveness and then later went to meet the IRA. He admitted that maybe he was naive, and he didn't get a very good response from them. Yet wasn't this exactly the sort of move that had to be made? And who is to say that it did not play some part in the peace process? First steps must be taken, even if they are rebuffed, or even if they appear foolish.

To think about... and do

Is there a relationship that needs to be mended in your life? Maybe a few steps towards somebody could make a huge difference—or even a phone call!

Mount Carmel:
From bloodshed to teaching peace

I KINGS 18:20–39

So Ahab sent to all the Israelites, and assembled the prophets at Mount Carmel. Elijah then came near to all the people, and said, 'How long will you go limping with two different opinions? If the Lord is God, follow him; but if Baal, then follow him.' ... They took the bull that was given them, prepared it, and called on the name of Baal from morning until noon, crying, 'O Baal, answer us!' But there was no voice, and no answer... At noon Elijah mocked them, saying, 'Cry aloud! Surely he is a god; either he is meditating, or he has wandered away, or he is on a journey, or perhaps he is asleep and must be awakened.'... The prophet Elijah came near and said, '... Answer me, O Lord, answer me, so that this people may know that you, O Lord, are God, and that you have turned their hearts back.' Then the fire of the Lord fell and consumed the burnt offering.

Today we are at Mount Carmel, at what is present day Haifa, and we start by looking at this struggle between Elijah and the prophets of Baal. It is the great struggle between monotheism and paganism and Elijah is trying to draw them away from Baal towards Yahweh. It is an extraordinary story, with Elijah goading the people and sarcastically suggesting that maybe their god is sleeping. The context is in a year of drought and so Elijah, drenching his sacrifice in water, suggests an almost priceless offering. He then prays a far more sober prayer than the prophets of Baal, and God hears his prayer. Elijah then has the prophets of Baal killed, talks to Ahab, and the drought ends.

It is a difficult story. Clearly the intention is that people should worship the true God and not a primitive, cultic god. On the other hand, the incident then ends with brutality, which still reflects a very primitive view of God. The New Testament shows an understanding of God that has developed from this view. God still rejects the worship of false idols, whether these are superstition, nationalism, wrong or inadequate understandings of God, racism, materialism or systems of domination, but God does not support one group against another—God is not a tribal God or a God who requires bloodshed. The blood of Christ has been shed and this is enough, and he is our peace.

There is an interesting aftermath to this story. Elijah has beaten the prophets of Baal, he has seen the end of the drought. He runs an extraordinary distance afterwards, and then he has news that Queen Jezebel wants to kill him. He is profoundly depressed and sits down under a tree and asks the Lord to take away his life. Despite the apparent success of the incident with the prophets of Baal, Elijah is deeply depressed. His strength is obviously low, so now he enters a time of sleeping and eating—good advice if we are depressed or run down—and then God speaks to him, not in the wind or in the earthquake, nor in the fire. But after the fire there is the sound of 'sheer silence'. It is a mysterious moment and Elijah senses the presence of God. It is good to take time to be silent, to try to discover God. Sometimes we try to work ourselves up in worship as if somehow this will attract God more, which seems a bit closer to the prophets of Baal! It's good to find time and a place to be silent and to allow God to meet us.

On the slopes of Mount Carmel today is Israel's chief port, Haifa. It is an important industrial, commercial and diamond centre with a population of 320,000. The Christian population is 17,000. Located in the middle of Haifa is St John's School, which provides pre-school through to secondary education for 390 boys and girls, both Christian and Muslim. The rector of St John's Evangelical Episcopal Church is the Revd Canon Shehadeh Shehadeh, and he carries out what he calls 'an aggressive programme of evangelism' in the only way possible in Israel, 'We make Jesus known to our students by our actions, and how we treat them, and how we teach them to treat each other. We teach them about forgiveness and salvation.' The school has been carrying out an exchange visit programme with a Jewish school, each school has visited the other and participated in a joint programme. The Hebron massacre was a setback, but the programme continues as love and trust are exchanged and built up. 'After the massacre, I just called them and assured them we loved them and cared for them,' Shehadeh said.

Talking of the current peace treaty, Dr Shehadeh said, 'We have to learn to teach peace. Signing a treaty is not peace. Peace starts with accepting each other at the lowest level. Peace is a process that takes a long time. We are all of the seed of Abraham and children of God.'

To pray about

Pray for the Christians of Haifa today. Remember Shehadeh Shehadeh and St John's Evangelical Episcopal Church and St John's School, and their work of peacemaking. Pray for the many other churches in

Haifa, which include the Orthodox, the Latin church, and also Hebrew believers. Pray for the Christian community... also pray for peacemakers and people of good will who are committed to the cause of justice in a selfless way, and pray that these steps towards peace will bear fruit.

Thought

False Idols

If we idolize wealth, then we create poverty.
If we idolize success, then we create the inadequate.
If we idolize power, we create powerlessness.

Journeying to peace with
Roni Ben Efrat, Jewish peacemaker

The long road to peace

Jewish peacemaker Roni Ben Efrat was born in Tel Aviv. She soon moved up into Upper Galilee as her parents were among the founders of the kibbutz Kfar Hanassi and soon after that they founded the agricultural village Kfar Mordechai. Roni is an active peacemaker who has suffered for her views, and been imprisoned. You can read her moving story in Janine di Giovanni's book, *Against the Stranger*. She was brought up in a protected, rarefied environment in which she had little contact with Palestinians. Yet, as she began to understand the story of her people, and to discover the story of the Palestinian people, she became strongly committed to the cause of justice. 'No honest person can agree with inflicting a disaster on another people because you were wronged. The problem Jews had in Europe had to be solved between them and the European community in the process of uprooting anti-Semitism.'

Roni has made her life a journey towards peace, which has often been costly and painful. When I met Roni, I was very impressed with her single-minded commitment to active peacemaking. As a Jew, she works for justice for the Palestinian people and works with other Jewish women to try and focus attention on the issues. She edits a magazine called *Challenge* which is not afraid to pursue truth and to tell some of the painful stories of what is happening at grassroots level to people who are losing their homes and being oppressed. Roni doesn't see easy answers. She says, 'It is difficult to know how many years it will take for creating a just solution. Nevertheless the long road we have to face, with new and unknown obstacles, cannot divert us from our essential cause, which is justice.' Roni and her friends, both Arab and Jewish, are involved in work in a village in western Galilee called Majd Al Krum, which is trying to empower Palestinian women through education in 'The Mothers' School'.

Week Six
Towards Jerusalem

If you look at the map, you see that Jesus goes on quite a journey now, from Galilee, presumably down the Jordan Valley to the northern part of the West Bank, which was called Samaria, down to Jericho. He then heads up the steep road from Jericho to Jerusalem, stopping at Bethany in preparation for his entrance into Jerusalem. Now one can feel the tempo pick up and the tension rising as Jesus 'sets his face to Jerusalem'. First he heads down through the West Bank, going through some of the towns and villages in the north—perhaps through Nablus (Shechem), pausing at Jacob's well in the southern part of Nablus. We'll pause here on our way down.

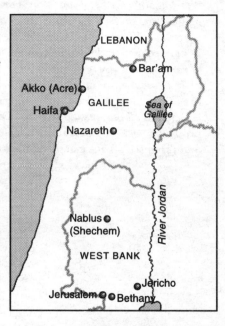

Jesus stopped here on his way back up to Galilee from Jerusalem on a previous occasion. Almost certainly he would have come to this well again because it is at a major fork in the road, and one branch heads west to Samaria and western Galilee, and the other goes north east towards Beth Shean and the Sea of Galilee, and it would be a natural stopping place for everyone. It is still a well that can be visited today, on the southern side of Nablus, and from the well there is an excellent view of Mount Gerizim.

Prayer: Father forgive us our divisions

Father, forgive us for we so readily divide your one human family into neat groups with convenient labels, forgetting that you are the Father of us all. For ourselves and all your children, we confess the ills of our present world; for this land, where group is set against group, is only a parable of our whole world: Catholics and Protestants are blind to the gifts you have given to each, the North builds barriers of commerce to protect itself from the poverty of the South, black and white approach each other with suspicious fear, and nation is set against nation.

Forgive us Father; that we use religion as a weapon, culture as a shield, and make the rich variety of human experience a wall of division. May we hear your Son, born and bred a Jew, speak to us again as he praises the goodness of a Samaritan traveller, receives a gift from a Samaritan woman by the well, shows compassion to a Roman soldier, and thus, in symbol, breaks down the false divisions of race, colour, sex and nationality behind which we still hide.

In his name, we affirm: we are members of one family, all women are our sisters, and men our brothers, we are parents to all children, children to all parents, kinsfolk to every race; and we will work, and pray, and serve until the unity which you created at the beginning, and promised for the end, is fulfilled in us. Amen.

Prayer by Donald Hilton, in *Pilgrim to the Holy Land*, published by McCrimmons

Setting his face

LUKE 9:51–56

When the days drew near for him to be taken up, he set his face to go to Jerusalem. And he sent messengers ahead of him. On their way they entered a village of the Samaritans to make ready for him; but they did not receive him, because his face was set toward Jerusalem. When his disciples James and John saw it, they said, 'Lord, do you want us to command fire to come down from heaven and consume them?' But he turned and rebuked them. Then they went on to another village.

So Jesus 'sets his face'. This is a unique expression which speaks of Jesus' obedience to do God's will, painful though it will be. And now we see him heading relentlessly towards Jerusalem, first of all through the Samaritan villages. Samaritans were not friendly to Jews, especially when they were heading on their way to Jerusalem because the Samaritans worshipped at Mount Gerizim, which they considered to be the right place for worship and for sacrifice. There are still two very small Samaritan communities, one is close to Nablus and the other is in a place called Holon, near Tel Aviv. As we know from the story of the Good Samaritan, the Samaritans were a much despised group of people. Their view that Mount Gerizim is the most holy site, rather than Jerusalem, brought them into conflict with the orthodox rabbis and, consequently, someone heading for Jerusalem as decisively as Jesus is doing is not someone they want to welcome, because he, in their eyes, represents a commitment to the 'other mountain'. James and John, 'the sons of thunder', are furious with the fact they are not accepted by the villagers and they want to call down fire. But Jesus will not accept this and rebukes them, because his way is not a way of revenge or domination or violence. It's interesting in Acts chapter 8 that when Philip headed down to Samaria and 'proclaimed the Messiah to them, the crowds with one accord listened eagerly'. So this part of the West Bank, which we don't hear a great deal about, later heard the 'good news' from Philip with great warmth and they accepted Jesus as their Messiah.

In some ways there are parallels with the present day situation. Jesus was going through an area where the people were not 'acceptable' for racial and religious reasons—that is still the case with the West Bank. It's an area that has suffered and longs to have its own autonomy. Meeting with Christians there, I found that very often they feel forgotten or ignored. I well remember a night in Zebabdeh, a little village up near Jenin. I did a concert at the local Anglican church and then spent the night in the home of a Palestinian family. That evening we were taken around, through the fields, and to different families and we felt a strong sense of community, and somehow their life did not seem so different from our biblical image of Palestine. We were welcomed by all, but heard painful stories, as they were under curfew at that time and could not get to their places of work. It was just after the Gulf War and they felt completely isolated and disheartened. They said that the most powerful armies in the world could be mobilized to stop Saddam Hussein but why was no one prepared to enforce the U.N. resolutions that said the occupiers must move from their land? The vicar of Zebabdeh, Bilal Habiby, took me down to Nablus, where he is also chaplain of the hospital, and we heard the stories of many of the people injured during the Intifada, people who are forgotten, people with no names, people with no passports.

It wasn't only the Samaritans that couldn't receive Jesus with his face set towards Jerusalem. We've seen that Peter couldn't, at Caesarea Philippi. For many people, the road of Jesus is not what they want. They want a different kind of king, a different kind of Lord, not one who is a servant and who goes to a cross. And straight after the passage that we've looked at today, Jesus warns people that would be followers that it's going to be hard because, 'Foxes have holes and birds of the air have nests; but the Son of Man has nowhere to lay his head' and he warns them that, 'No one who puts a hand to the plough and looks back is fit for the kingdom of God.' It's a hard road, it's a committed road, it's a way of crucifixion, but it's a way onwards to resurrection.

Prayer

So now you've set your face, you know the route you must take,
against the odds, against people's wishes… towards Jerusalem…
towards a cross. But it's also towards resurrection, and we pray
that we will be people who walk in your footsteps, giving ourselves to
others, and being part of your community of hope. In your name.
Amen.

A meeting by the well

JOHN 4:5–14

*He came to a Samaritan city called Sychar, near the plot of ground that
Jacob had given to his son Joseph. Jacob's well was there, and Jesus,
tired out by his journey, was sitting by the well. It was about noon. A
Samaritan woman came to draw water, and Jesus said to her, 'Give
me a drink.' (His disciples had gone to the city to buy food.) The
Samaritan woman said to him, 'How is it that you, a Jew, ask a drink
of me, a woman of Samaria?' (Jews do not share things in common
with Samaritans.) Jesus answered her, 'If you knew the gift of God,
and who it is that is saying to you, "Give me a drink," you would have
asked him, and he would have given you living water.' The woman said
to him, 'Sir, you have no bucket and the well is deep. Where do you get
that living water? Are you greater than our ancestor Jacob, who gave
us the well, and with his sons and his flocks drank from it?' Jesus said
to her, 'Everyone who drinks of this water will be thirsty again, but
those who drink of the water that I will give them will never be thirsty.'*

Jesus is a friend of women in the Bible, sometimes breaking the custom of
the day by being so. This is the case in this passage and when the disciples
come back, 'They were astonished that he was speaking with a woman.' Jesus
valued women and respected them, and even likens God to a woman, for
example in the parable of the woman and the lost coin.

This is not only a woman, but a Samaritan, someone of the wrong racial or
religious grouping. He starts the conversation, and she is amazed, because
Jews would not consider sharing a water pot with Samaritans—it would be
unclean. Now Jesus starts to teach her about the water of life. She is shocked
and she says, 'Can you do better than providing a well like Jacob?' And Jesus
points out that he is greater than Jacob, just as later he will suggest that he
is greater than Abraham.

Jesus then tells her to go and call her husband and we discover that she
hasn't a husband currently, but that she has apparently had five husbands and
the person she is living with now is not her husband. The woman is taken
aback at Jesus' insight and so takes the opportunity to ask a religious

question about the difference between the Samaritans and the Jews—where should we worship? Jesus points out that the place of worship is not important, the important thing is to worship 'in spirit and truth'.

Here Jesus affirms someone in the very fact of breaking customs and talking with her. At the same time he points to the living water that he brings and she comes to see him as the Messiah. By refusing to say that she's unclean, either as a woman or because of her race or religion, he wins another follower. By refusing to be exclusive, he gives a further insight into the nature of the values of the kingdom of God.

Mrs Cedar Duaybis is a Palestinian Episcopalian who works for the Jerusalem YWCA. She is particularly concerned with women's issues in church and society. She comments on this encounter at the well:

The story of Jesus and the Samaritan woman has always fascinated me, especially after living for fourteen years in Nablus... We were an Anglican pastor's family. Every time I entered our church, St Philip's, I read above the altar that verse, imparted to the woman of Samaria during that brief, yet so rich encounter Jesus had with her: 'God is spirit, and they that worship him must worship him in spirit and in truth.' Nothing short of a complete change in attitude satisfied him. It was not so-called 'holy places' he cared for. It was people and their attitude towards God and each other that concerned him, for when that is correct, everything else falls into place.

Our time in Nablus was a very challenging one. It was there that I learnt what it was like to feel my knees turn to water at the sound of Israeli soldiers' boots on our doorstep, or my mouth go dry as they searched the house for I never knew what. It was there that the term 'tongue-tied' became real, and I thought my twelve-year-old daughter would never speak again. It was there that we saw our teenage son completely broken, unable to take any more and seeking release from life. It was there that I stood shivering alongside my neighbour, as she first laid eyes on the bullet-ridden body of her seventeen-year-old daughter, and I tried in vain to comfort her. It was in Nablus that we, as a family, wrestled with our faith. We tried to pull ourselves through and help others along the way... There was a conflict raging inside me between the Palestinian, the Christian, and the woman. But, through the mediation of the gospel, my peace process had begun. The tripartite meeting took place; peace and harmony won, and a Palestinian Christian woman become one whole person.

From *Faith and the Intifada*, Orbis Books, 1992

Prayer

Lord—make us whole—give us this water so that we may never be thirsty. Amen.

Wednesday of week 6
Blindness and sight

Luke 18:31–43

Then he took the twelve aside and said to them, 'See, we are going up to Jerusalem, and everything that is written about the Son of Man by the prophets will be accomplished. For he will be handed over to the Gentiles; and he will be mocked and insulted and spat upon. After they have flogged him, they will kill him, and on the third day he will rise again.' But they understood nothing about all these things; in fact, what he said was hidden from them, and they did not grasp what was said.

As he approached Jericho, a blind man was sitting by the roadside begging. When he heard a crowd going by, he asked what was happening. They told him, 'Jesus of Nazareth is passing by.' Then he shouted, 'Jesus, Son of David, have mercy on me!' Those who were in front sternly ordered him to be quiet; but he shouted even more loudly, 'Son of David, have mercy on me!' Jesus stood still and ordered the man to be brought to him; and when he came near, he asked him, 'What do you want me to do for you?' He said, 'Lord, let me see again.' Jesus said to him, 'Receive your sight; your faith has saved you.' Immediately he regained his sight and followed him, glorifying God.

Jesus makes his third prediction in Luke of his death and resurrection, but the disciples don't understand it—they are, in a sense, blind. Luke shows the disciples as unable to see—'What he said was hidden from them.' Now, as we approach Jericho, there is a blind man who, in a way, sees. He certainly believes Jesus can heal him, and he is aware that Jesus is the Son of David. Jesus' reputation has gone before him. And when he gets his sight back, the blind man follows, praising God.

Maybe the disciples are reeling because they are hearing too much from Jesus. Today's passage comes just after Jesus has spoken to the rich young ruler and he says to the disciples, 'How hard it is for those who have wealth to enter the kingdom of God!' They exclaim, 'Then who can be saved?' The view was held that wealth was a sign of blessing from God. There are some groups today that still hold this view. And Jesus is turning this idea on its head, showing that in the kingdom of God wealth is not a sign of blessing.

Indeed, you may be called to give up your wealth to follow the simple path, just as happened to that other rich young ruler, Francis of Assisi. Then Peter says, 'Well, at least we've given up things for your sake, so we should be all right.' Jesus doesn't put him down, he points out that that's true—maybe meaning that he'll have the benefits of the fellowship of the church and being part of that community in this life. Then, having encouraged him, comes our passage for today, 'I'm off to die and rise again.' It's all very bewildering, this upside-down kingdom. This Jesus, with his surprising stories and teaching, is always catching them off their guard.

So we are poised outside Jericho—the city of palms—before the last walk up the desert road to Jerusalem, and a blind man has seen whilst the truth is hidden from Jesus' disciples. Tomorrow we will find someone else who sees and whose life is completely changed, and who can accept the challenge of Jesus in a way the rich young ruler could not.

To think about

Jericho is in some ways a place of hope as the Palestinian flags fly all around it. It's a symbol of a new country, and new possibilities. Not without its frustrations, at the moment it is a small area and a long way from the rest of Palestine—i.e. Gaza. But it's like a sign of the possibility of better things to come. Pray for the people of Jericho, that the city of palms will also be a city of peace, and of first fruits of autonomy for the people of the West Bank.

Prayer

Lord, as we walk with you now, from Jericho to Jerusalem, past the place of your temptation, maybe we are tempted not to be your companions. Give us the courage to live your gospel and show your light. May we be those whose eyes are open to your way, your truth, and your life. Amen.

Two changed lives

LUKE 19:1–10

He entered Jericho and was passing through it. A man was there named Zacchaeus; he was a chief tax collector and was rich. He was trying to see who Jesus was, but on account of the crowd he could not, because he was short in stature. So he ran ahead and climbed a sycamore tree to see him, because he was going to pass that way. When Jesus came to the place, he looked up and said to him, 'Zacchaeus, hurry and come down; for I must stay at your house today.' So he hurried down and was happy to welcome him. All who saw it began to grumble and said, 'He has gone to be the guest of one who is a sinner.' Zacchaeus stood there and said to the Lord, 'Look, half of my possessions, Lord, I will give to the poor; and if I have defrauded anyone of anything, I will pay him back four times as much.' Then Jesus said to him, 'Today salvation has come to this house, because he too is a son of Abraham. For the Son of Man came to seek out and to save the lost.'

Jesus now enters Jericho and he comes across another rich man, this time a tax collector, Zacchaeus. Being a tax collector, and cooperating with the occupying forces, he would have been considered unclean. Yet curiously enough, the name Zacchaeus means 'clean'. He longed to see Jesus and had climbed up the sycamore tree, and when Jesus affirms him, and breaks the barriers of what is 'clean' and 'unclean', by saying he is going to come to his house, he is overwhelmed. Not surprisingly, people grumble or murmur because Jesus is crossing boundaries and breaking rules. But Zacchaeus instantly understands the implications of the gospel. He will give away half his possessions to the poor, and where he has defrauded, he will pay back four times as much. Following Jesus has implications for how we live.

Earlier the disciples had wondered who could be saved, if it was so hard for a rich person to enter the kingdom of God; this passage gives the answer. If you radically change and become a follower of Jesus, there is salvation. Nobody is beyond the pale and unable to be one of God's chosen people. Jesus the shepherd has come to seek out and to save those who are lost and to welcome them home.

This should influence our own understanding of evangelism. We are not out on the attack: we are to welcome people, so they see God's love reaching out to them. One of the key issues that impacted Zaccheus was that he was considered as clean and acceptable to Jesus.

The way of Jesus is inclusive, rather than exclusive. Lynda Brayer was particularly attracted to the Christian gospel through this point, and through reading Paul, whom she considered her Jewish brother. Lynda came from a traditional Jewish upbringing in South Africa, with a strongly Zionist background. She emigrated to Israel where, as an Israeli lawyer, she found herself increasingly involved in cases arising from Israel's anti-missionary law and restrictions affecting the work and residence of Christian foreign nationals employed by Christian agencies working in Jerusalem. Gradually she also became involved in other cases affecting Palestinians, who were connected to these Christians. Then she started to explore the theology of the Christian gospel. She was baptized as a Christian in 1988 and says, 'I don't mind being controversial. Judaism does not reach out for everybody. The particularity of Judaism is it's fatal flaw.' Lynda now works with the Society of St Yves, and she describes the work as a 'natural product of the mission statement of the Church'. Committed to preaching 'good news to the poor', she sees that the Church has no choice other than to identify with the poor and the oppressed, who in the political context of the Holy Land are primarily the Palestinian population of the Occupied Territories. She sees life under military law as the equivalent of 'being treated as an object rather than a person'. Lynda has spotted the very thing which Jesus was pointing out to Zacchaeus, that people are not objects, nor are they unclean, but they are valuable and worthwhile. As she carries out the gospel mandate, she is trying to assert the worth and value of all people. Hers is a changed life, just as Zacchaeus' life was changed. We can't expect to follow the way of Jesus and not change.

To think about

The process of change can sometimes be sudden like it was for Zacchaeus, but it is also an ongoing work, as God brings us closer to his ways, his attitudes and his style of life. Zacchaeus changed because of Jesus coming to his house. Imagine Jesus with you today in your house. Are there certain things in your way of life you would want to change because they don't reflect the values of his kingdom?

Lament over Jerusalem

LUKE 19:41–42; MATTHEW 23:37

As he came near and saw the city, he wept over it, saying, 'If you, even you, had only recognized on this day the things that make for peace! But now they are hidden from your eyes.'

'Jerusalem, Jerusalem, the city that kills the prophets and stones those who are sent to it! How often have I desired to gather your children together as a hen gathers her brood under her wings, and you were not willing!'

As I sat looking across at Jerusalem last year from the little chapel of Dominus Flevit, which means 'the Lord wept', I thought about these words: 'If you had only recognized the things that make for peace.' The group I was with began to discuss the significance of this. The little chapel is designed like a tear-drop, half-way up the Mount of Olives, and it is an ideal site for meditation. Somehow there seemed something so contemporary about Jesus weeping and longing for peace—one still wants to approach Jerusalem in the same way.

The very word 'Jerusalem' means 'City of Peace' and yet this city has seen an extraordinary amount of bloodshed. In 1099 when the crusaders came and killed both Muslim and Jew, 'men rode in blood up to their knees and bridle reins' (Krey, *The First Crusade*, page 261, quoted in K. Armstrong, *Holy War*). It is a city that has been invaded nearly forty times. It is a city that is seen as the capital by two communities—the Palestinians and the Jews—and three religions see it as a special place—Christianity, Judaism and Islam. If peace were to come here, it would be a sign of hope for the whole world. Just as peace in South Africa has motivated others to start searching for peace, so peace in Jerusalem would have a worldwide impact. We are poised on the verge of Holy Week, and everything we have been learning—from the Nazareth manifesto through to the new law of the Sermon on the Mount, from the manner of Jesus' birth to the manner of his entry into Jerusalem (which we will see next week)—points to a way 'that makes for peace'.

Ched Myers in his book, *Binding the Strong Man*, which is a commentary on St Mark's Gospel, says this, 'Jesus' long march to Jerusalem, during which he instructed his followers in the way of the cross and non-violence, takes Mark's story from the margins of Palestinian society to its centre. Jesus prepares to enter Jerusalem, not as a reverent pilgrim coming to demonstrate his allegiance to the temple state, but as a subversive prophet challenging the foundations of state power.' It's important to realize that Jesus is opposing the ways of domination and power that have caused the pain of Jerusalem. Too often as pilgrims, we sit there reverently but we need to dwell on what are the 'things that make for peace' which are all too easily hidden from our eyes. They are the things that break the walls of division, and in Matthew the cry of Jesus is: 'Jerusalem, city of peace, the city that kills the prophets and kills those that are sent to it.' This city of peace had a reputation for violence even then. It will kill another prophet, but it can never silence the message of peace that he comes to bring.

As we focus today on Jesus' prayer for Jerusalem, take time to focus on yourself, and any attitude that sustains bigotry or intolerance. If we are not dealing with the bitterness in our own lives, then we are not able to be peacemakers on a wider level. Jerusalem is a warning to Christians, not only the horror of 1099, but even when Christians were shown generosity, they did not want to show it to others. For instance, in AD636, the Muslim period of Jerusalem began with a peaceful take over by Caliph 'Umar. He gave Christians access to the holy sites and freedom of worship and they pleaded with him to keep the Jews out, but he wouldn't agree and gave the same concession to the Jews. Later on the Christians expelled Orthodox groups that they believed to be heretical. When they ruled, as conquerors in the city, they forbade Jews and Muslims access at certain periods. None of this is the way of Jesus. We are to serve others and to reject the ways of bigotry and intolerance. BBC correspondent Gerald Butt has a lovely prayer for peace in the Holy Land.

A prayer for peace in the Holy Land

O Lord soften the stone hearts
of those who preach and practise
intolerance and bigotry;
as the sun's setting glow
softens the stone walls of your Holy City, Jerusalem.

Lord, the rocky hills, the valleys,
the deserts and the sea shores
are filled with the echoes of
centuries of pain.

Lord, bring peace to house and village.
Comfort the mothers who fret and those who mourn.
Lord, keep strong the twisted old root
of the olive tree, and protect the young vine.

Lord of water and stone,
of bread and wine,
Lord of resurrection,
feed hope, and bring peace,
to this wracked but beautiful Holy Land.

Gerald Butt

A pause at Bethany

JOHN 12:1-8

Six days before the Passover Jesus came to Bethany, the home of
Lazarus, whom he had raised from the dead. There they gave a dinner
for him. Martha served, and Lazarus was one of those at the table with
him. Mary took a pound of costly perfume made of pure nard, anointed
Jesus' feet, and wiped them with her hair. The house was filled with the
fragrance of the perfume. But Judas Iscariot, one of the disciples (the
one who was about to betray him), said, 'Why was this perfume not
sold for three hundred denarii and the money given to the poor?'...
Jesus said, 'Leave her alone. She bought it so that she might keep it for
the day of my burial. You always have the poor with you, but you do
not always have me.'

Jesus has now walked up the rocky mountainous road and he is just outside
Jerusalem. In John's Gospel, we get the sense of a pause. Jesus is with his
friends. It seems to be the home where he most liked to be—with Mary,
Martha and Lazarus. And Mary, we are told, takes costly perfume and anoints
his feet and wipes them with her hair. It is a most extravagant gesture.

In Mark's Gospel, the incident also occurs at Bethany, though in a
different house, the house of Simon the leper, and we are not told who the
woman was who anointed Jesus' feet. In Luke's Gospel it had happened
earlier, up in Galilee when he was eating at the house of a Pharisee, and a
woman—who was a 'sinner'—wept 'and began to bathe his feet with her tears
and wipe them with her hair. Then she continued kissing his feet and
anointing them with the ointment.' Unless women were regularly in the habit
of doing this to Jesus, it seems more likely that John is making use of an
incident that has already happened and he is placing it before the Passover to
bring out its full significance. It is, in a sense, a preparation for the day of
Jesus' burial, and an anointing for the hour that is to come. Maybe this is
what prompts Jesus to think of washing the disciples' feet later in the week—
clearly he is very moved by the incident. It seems a very intimate act that is
both a prophetic preparation for his burial and also a sign of affection.

Maybe there's something of the idea of the anointing of a king in this incident. Jesus is about to ride into Jerusalem, just as king David had done, and David was anointed by Samuel in preparation for that. As Jesus turns upside-down all the ideas of kingship, perhaps this anointing of his feet is an almost literal 'turning upside-down' of anointing.

Mary's act is extravagant—a beautiful deed. Judas is irritated by it and says, 'This money could have been given to the poor', and John has no intention of allowing Judas to have any honourable motives behind this comment. But, nevertheless, it's a fair discussion and one that has gone on throughout history. Should we spend our money on something beautiful for God when there are so many poor and hungry? When I visited Mother Teresa's home for children in Calcutta, I was moved to see the phrase 'Something beautiful for God' painted over the front of the building. She sees her deed of rescuing unwanted children as something beautiful for God. If we do extravagant gestures for God without caring for the poor and needy within our community, we deny the very message that he came to proclaim. There is always a task to be done to show love to the poor. There is also a place to do an act of worship, a spontaneous gesture, a work of art, that is both a loving and prophetic act like this one.

Meditation: Tomorrow the Kidron Valley

Tomorrow the Kidron Valley.

Today a time with friends—rest in Bethany.
Always heading to Jerusalem—face set that way—towards
*   Jerusalem.*
All the long wilderness climb from Jericho.
Face set towards Jerusalem.
No doubt remembering the temptations in the wilderness as you
*   walked the wilderness road.*
Face set towards Jerusalem—but now the temptation is not to
*   go there, not to drink the cup.*
And Bethany is—friends and rest—the lull before the storm.

Tomorrow the Kidron Valley.

Today is laughter and reminiscing and eating and drinking and
*   drawing strength from friends and rest.*

Tomorrow the Kidron Valley.

Someone realized how precious the moment and showed how much
she loved you and valued you, and it was good because...

Tomorrow the Kidron Valley.

Someone washed your feet and served you and it felt good—
later that week you would wash feet too.
And so to bed and rest in the home of friends—a quiet prayer—
maybe 'sufficient unto the day is the evil thereof' because...

Tomorrow the Kidron Valley.

With the dawn—the rest is over—face set towards Jerusalem
again—there's a knock on the door.
Someone is there with a donkey.

Today the Kidron Valley.
Today Jerusalem.
Face set to Jerusalem.

Garth Hewitt, April 1995

Palm Sunday
From Ptolemais (Acco) to Bar'am

ACTS 21:7–8

When we had finished the voyage from Tyre, we arrived at Ptolemais;
and we greeted the believers and stayed with them for one day. The
next day we left and came to Caesarea: and we went into the house of
Philip the evangelist, one of the seven, and stayed with him.

Today we join Paul and Luke at Acco or Acre, or what in the Bible is called
Ptolemais. Maybe Jesus visited here but we have no record of it, yet already
when Paul and Luke arrived here there were believers with whom they stayed
for one day. The next day they carried on down the coast and went to
Caesarea and met up with Philip. Paul was *en route* to Jerusalem and, in fact,
when he stayed at Philip's house a prophet called Agabus came and
prophesied that he would be taken prisoner in Jerusalem. The people wept
and urged him not to go—perhaps reminiscent of Peter's response to Jesus
when he says he must go to Jerusalem—and Paul answered, 'What are you
doing, weeping and breaking my heart? For I am ready not only to be bound
but even to die in Jerusalem for the name of the Lord Jesus.' So Paul had 'set
his face' towards Jerusalem, and Luke adds, 'Since he would not be
persuaded, we remained silent except to say, "The Lord's will be done" '—a
little passage reminiscent of Jesus's own prayer in the Garden of
Gethsemane.

On my first visit to Acco (Acre), I was taken by Elias Chacour, who acted
as my guide, and pointed out that there was a Chacour who had helped to
build the walls of the old city. We visited the subterranean crusader city,
where excavations have revealed a vast complex of crusader buildings. We also
visited the Al Jezzar mosque where Elias introduced me to one of the Muslim
religious leaders and I experienced something of the close cooperation that
exists between Christians and Muslims so often in this part of the world. Also
there was a caravansari called Khan Al-Umdan (Khan of the pillars). This is
an extraordinary place, like an old-style motel. Underneath you would have
put your animals in the stables that surround the courtyard, then you would
have stayed in the rooms on the upper level. So it's a fascinating place for
tourists to visit, and it still has its Christian communities.

From there I was taken up to the Lebanese border by Elias. This was a journey across northern Galilee to a place called Bar'am. This was the village where Elias was brought up, and he showed me the fig tree where he was playing, as a young lad, when the Israeli soldiers arrived. He had been told by his father that the Israelis were coming and that they must welcome them, but when they came it was with guns and Elias and his family were driven out of their village. Later, they were told they could come back—on Christmas Day—and as they came over the brow of the hill, their village was shelled. The ruins remain there to this day, including the church, which is the only undamaged building. Some of Elias' people had disappeared and he was the one who, as a young lad playing a game of football, stumbled on the shallow grave, which let them know what had happened to these people—they had been massacred. Instead of being a bitter person, however, he has committed his life to walking in the footsteps of Jesus and being a person of peace.

Today if you go to Bar'am, you will see that there is an Israeli tourist plaque there, claiming the place as a site of antiquities. In fact it refers to an old synagogue which is there, and no reference is made to the village of Bar'am. You will have to pay to go in, though if you are with Elias Chacour, he will steadfastly refuse to do this. If you pass the site of the synagogue, turn left and you will come into the ruined village of Bar'am, clearly seeing the church with its bell on top, and the rest of the village is now overgrown and not nearly as visible as when I first saw it. The extraordinary story of this village and of the life of Elias Chacour is told in his books, *Blood Brothers* and *We Belong to the Land*. It's a life of hope, committed to the gospel but walking the painful and rarely comfortable road towards peace.

Say No To Peace

Say no to peace
If what they mean by peace
Is the quiet misery of hunger,
The frozen stillness of fear,
The silence of broken spirits,
The unborn hopes of the oppressed.

Tell them that peace
Is the shouting of children at play,
The babble of tongues set free,
The thunder of dancing feet,
And a father's voice singing.

Say no to peace
If what they mean by peace
Is a rampart of gleaming missiles,
The arming of distant wars,
Money at ease in its castle,
And grateful poor at the gate.

Tell them that peace
Is the hauling down of flags,
The forging of guns into ploughs,
The giving of fields to the landless,
And hunger a fading dream.

Brian Wren, from *Praising a Mystery*,
Hope Publishing Company, 1986,
copyright Oxford University Press

Jerusalem

A prayer for Jerusalem

*Our heavenly Father, who
allowed us to live in this city
where your beloved Son was
crucified and raised from the
dead, make us worthy of its
heavenly message. We pray that
the holy places will turn us to the
things that deepen our faith and
renew us in the hope of
everlasting life.*

*We beseech you Lord, you know what the people of this holy city have
suffered, and are suffering: up-rootedness, lostness, the pain of being torn
apart in separation, the pain of unsettlement, the pain of death.*

We beseech you Lord to give this holy city Peace built on Justice.

*We beseech you Lord to give the people of this city calm in their souls, and
courage in their hearts.*

Strengthen O God, the hearts of those who work to bring Justice.

*Bless their efforts and make them succeed over the powers of evil, and
value and support them with your Holy Spirit.*

*Help us God, as we pass through such difficult trials, that we may grow to
know your truth, that we may witness to you our Saviour, by our lives.*

*May the way of the cross be the one we choose for ourselves, that each will
carry his cross to follow you, Shepherd of our souls, Teacher, crucified and
raised from the dead. Amen.*

Najwa Farah, from *Palestinian Pain and
Promise*, Christians Aware, 1990

Journeying to peace with
Canon Naim Ateek

Seeking peace and pursuing it

So with Jesus we enter Jerusalem... In Jerusalem, if you visit St George's Anglican Cathedral, attend the 9.30 Eucharist for the Arabic-speaking congregation. Canon Naim Ateek, the pastor, spots visitors and gives a synopsis of his sermon in English. He describes himself as 'a Christian, a Palestinian, an Arab and an Israeli'! He is the author of the book, *Justice, and Only Justice* and has been a constant campaigner for peace.

Naim was born in Beisan (Beth Shean) a town in southern Galilee, or in Jesus' time, one of the towns of the Decapolis. His father came from Nablus, and his family name, Ateek, is from the Arabic word *atiq* which means 'old' or 'ancient'. A few years ago he met one of the leaders of the Samaritan community in Nablus, and it turned out he had been a classmate of Naim's father during their early childhood. He told Naim that the name Ateek signifies that their family was one of the oldest Christian Arab families in Nablus, which filled Naim with great joy and pride, because who knows how far those roots go back? Although they have those long roots, more recently they have felt rootless. The family had move to Beisan and it was here that Naim grew up until in 1948 the Israeli soldiers came and forced them out at gunpoint. So, like 750,000 others, they became refugees, and ended up in Nazareth.

Naim now acts as convenor of the Palestinian Liberation Theology Group, Sabeel, and edits their magazine, *Cornerstone*. In this magazine he writes about the way powerful leaders who visit Jerusalem, 'come with the illusion that the answers to peace lie with the Herods in Jerusalem'. But, he says, it would be better for 'today's Magi to visit Bethlehem. They do not realize that the genuine answers to peace lie in everything that the child of Bethlehem has stood for; humility, openness, love of others, forgiveness, even sacrifice of oneself for others. We are part of the people of Jerusalem today. The child of Bethlehem has inspired us. We humbly seek to be his followers, guided and motivated by his Spirit. We try to communicate his message and carry on a prophetic ministry as he had done.'

On a donkey—the rejection of power

MATTHEW 21:1–11:

When they had come near Jerusalem and had reached Bethphage, at the Mount of Olives, Jesus sent two disciples, saying to them, 'Go into the village ahead of you, and immediately you will find a donkey tied, and a colt with her; untie them and bring them to me. If anyone says anything to you, just say this, "The Lord needs them." And he will send them immediately.' This took place to fulfil what had been spoken through the prophet, saying, 'Tell the daughter of Zion, Look, your king is coming to you, humble, and mounted on a donkey, and on a colt, the foal of a donkey.' The disciples went and did as Jesus had directed them; they brought the donkey and the colt, and put their cloaks on them, and he sat on them. A very large crowd spread their cloaks on the road, and others cut branches from the trees and spread them on the road. The crowds that went ahead of him and that followed were shouting, 'Hosanna to the Son of David! Blessed is the one who comes in the name of the Lord! Hosanna in the highest heaven!' When he entered Jerusalem, the whole city was in turmoil, asking, 'Who is this?' The crowds were saying, 'This is the prophet Jesus from Nazareth in Galilee.'

Jesus spent much of his time, when he was teaching, talking in parables. Now, he acts out a parable. No riding on a war horse, even though the crowds rightly discern that this is the Son of David, the great warrior king. But Jesus comes rejecting the way of war and violence, 'See your king—gentle and riding on a donkey,' says Matthew, quoting from Zechariah. Ched Myers, in his book, *Binding the Strong Man*, says, that the so-called 'triumphal entry' is 'a misnomer and is carefully choreographed political street theatre designed to repudiate "messianic triumphalism."'

So, here we have Jesus—a king after David—but a king who brings peace. He reminds us of a quotation that is used so often at Christmas-time, Isaiah 9:6–7, 'Wonderful Counsellor... Prince of Peace. His authority shall grow continually, and there shall be endless peace for the throne of David and his kingdom. He will establish and uphold it with justice and with righteousness from this time onward and forevermore.' His kingdom is so different. It is marked by peace, by wholeness, by doing justice, by right living. It's the place where inequalities are destroyed.

Maybe we are not always happy with the style and the methods of Jesus. Gerard W. Hughes, in his book, *God of Surprises* says this:

The love of God for us and all creation is being revealed in the sufferings of Christ. We are called to answer this love, not by passive suffering but by letting the love and compassion of God and his hunger for justice express itself in our own lives. If we enter into the Passion of Christ, we begin to feel the pain of this world as Christ did, and his Spirit at work in us takes this pain, absorbs it and answers it with forgiveness and love. We would prefer a different kind of God, a God who would hurl back the pain onto those who inflicted it, adding a bit more to deter them from ever trying the same again, but 'God's foolishness is wiser than human wisdom, and God's weakness is stronger than human strength' (1 Corinthians 1:25). Yes, we might be tempted to call down fire, like the 'sons of thunder', but the gentle successor to David—gentle and riding on a donkey—says, 'Don't be afraid.' For those who are raw with their hurts—the victims of wrong relationships, he rejects the worldly way of solving problems, with its violence and its power, and he brings a better way.

I asked Naim Ateek what has been his motivation. He replied, 'I would say definitely the words of Christ—"Blessed are the peacemakers for they shall be called children of God." I think those words, probably more than any other, are what really keep me going, knowing that if I am doing the work of peacemaking, then I am really behaving as a child of God—that's it, that's the bottom line. It's always difficult because being a peacemaker in our situation is also being a justice maker, and most governments like to talk about peace but they don't want to talk about justice because, for them, peace is keeping the status quo... We cry over the well-being of the city of Jerusalem that does not know "the things that make for peace" as he had done... We have a vision for peace that is inspired by faith in God and love and concern for all.'

Thought

Behold your king, gentle and riding on a donkey.

Turning the tables—the rejection of exploitation

LUKE 19:45–48

Then he entered the temple and began to drive out those who were selling things there; and he said, 'It is written, "My house shall be a house of prayer"; but you have made it a den of robbers.' Every day he was teaching in the temple. The chief priests, the scribes and the leaders of the people kept looking for a way to kill him; but they did not find anything they could do, for all the people were spellbound by what they heard.

Jesus now comes to the temple, the centre of Jewish spirituality. It is a significant stop on his journey and he becomes like a prophet from the Old Testament. As he turns the tables, he quotes from Jeremiah 7:11—in this chapter Jeremiah is told by God to stand in the gate of the Lord's house and tell the people that, unless they mend their ways, there will be judgment on the temple. But he then goes on to say, 'If you truly amend your ways and your doings, if you truly act justly one with another, if you do not oppress the alien, the orphan, and the widow, or shed innocent blood in this place, and if you do not go after other gods to your own hurt, then I will dwell with you in this place.' He adds, 'Will you steal, murder, commit adultery, swear falsely, make offerings to Ba'al, and go after other gods that you have not known, and then come and stand before me in this house, which is called by my name, and say, "We are safe!"—only to do all these abominations?' He then asks the question that Jesus quotes, 'Has this house become a den of robbers?' The Old Testament prophets are often challenging the worshipping community in the name of God, because they are allowing immoral behaviour or injustice to flourish, whilst at the same time, trying to worship God. In other words, they are not living out the worship in their lives, they are inconsistent. And God can't stand a mockery made of worship. If you come through the gates to worship, then certain actions are required.

So here is Jesus, like one of those prophets of the Old Testament, turning the tables of hypocrisy—of lives that don't match up, turning the tables of those who exploit, those who use power wrongly, those who manipulate, who love money, those who are greedy and yet claim to be worshippers. Jesus is saying if you are a worshipper, it encompasses all of life, it's a revolution of justice, love, wholeness and purity.

Jesus also turns the tables of racial superiority. As we see from the Jeremiah passage, we are not to oppress the alien or the immigrant in our society by making them second-class citizens. The fact that we imprison people who come to our country as refugees asking for asylum, and we imprison them with absolutely no trial and no recourse to normal legal representation is an unjust act. This, in my view, is not acceptable. These tables need to be turned. We need to assert the worth and value of all human beings. Stephen Lawrence, an eighteen-year-old black youth, was killed on his way home one night in 1994. Some white youths attacked him and beat him up. He staggered down the road and collapsed, just outside the Catholic church, where two people emerged who had been at a prayer meeting. They found him on the street. They didn't know who he was, or what had happened, but they could see he was badly injured so they knelt beside him and stayed with him. They tried to find some words of hope to say and they kept repeating, 'You are loved, you are loved.' It seems to me, they found the most valuable words. We need to repeat them to one another in our communities so walls of division are not allowed to be built up, and tables are turned against false racial superiority. We need one another, we need to affirm one another.

Jesus came riding into Jerusalem yesterday, gentle and unthreatening, the saviour for the raw and the hurt, the poor and the oppressed. Today we see his anger at those who exploit. Luke is quoting a passage from Isaiah 56 which says, 'My house shall be called a house of prayer *for all peoples*'—Mark includes these words in his version of the passage. This is not to be some exclusive place, but it's to be inclusive, a place for all nations, for the immigrant, for the dispossessed, for all. It will become a house of prayer, a place of joy. It's a wonderful picture of what the new community should be, what the new Israel should be.

Prayer

Lord, forgive us when we accept worldly attitudes that devalue others or exploit their vulnerability. Give us your heart, your mind, your eyes, and your love. Teach us to give a welcome to the lonely, to speak up for those without a voice and to stand up for the weak, and may our lives be marked by your joy as we serve others. Amen.

Washing the disciples' feet—
the way of the servant

JOHN 13:1–14

Now before the festival of the Passover, Jesus knew that his hour had come to depart from this world and go to the Father. Having loved his own who were in the world, he loved them to the end... And during supper Jesus... got up from the table, took off his outer robe, and tied a towel around himself. Then he poured water into a basin and began to wash the disciples' feet and to wipe them with the towel that was tied around him. He came to Simon Peter, who said to him, 'Lord, are you going to wash my feet?' Jesus answered, 'You do not know now what I am doing, but later you will understand.' Peter said to him, 'You will never wash my feet.' Jesus answered, 'Unless I wash you, you have no share with me.' Simon Peter said to him, 'Lord, not my feet only but also my hands and my head!' Jesus said to him, 'One who has bathed does not need to wash, except for the feet, but is entirely clean. ... he said to them, 'Do you know what I have done to you? You call me Teacher and Lord—and you are right, for that is what I am. So if I, your Lord and Teacher, have washed your feet, you also ought to wash one another's feet.'

Now we join Jesus at the Passover meal—a day early, but that's so that we can spend time on it tomorrow as well. Jesus wants to teach a vital lesson to the disciples as his time on earth is drawing to an end. The very timing of this feet-washing incident—given the urgency of Jesus' own timetable at this point—tells us something about its importance. There is no doubt the incident is a shock. Peter's reaction is normal. Jesus is fulfilling the role that a slave might fulfil when there is a visiting dignitary, and Peter is appalled. But Jesus is firm with him and says, 'Unless I wash you, you have no share with me.' Peter then has a typical over-enthusiastic response and says virtually 'wash all of me'. Jesus insists that he must serve his disciples, that is his nature, and that is the lesson, the acted parable, that he is teaching.

Verse 3 is intriguing. 'Jesus knew that the Father had put all things under his power—so he got up' (NIV). The feet-washing is a sign of his power. This is a profound truth. God's way of power is though serving, through giving and, of course, most profoundly, by giving himself on the cross. But it also reminds us that we are the servant Church, and we, too, are called to follow the way of the servant and the way of the cross. 'If anyone would come after me, he must deny himself and take up his cross and follow me.' Jesus clearly models himself on the servant in Isaiah who has a gentleness of spirit and who will bring forth justice to the nations. 'He will not cry or lift up his voice, or make it heard in the street; a bruised reed he will not break, and a dimly burning wick he will not quench; he will faithfully bring forth justice.' This is the servant whose gentle spirit will lift people up. He won't crush or dominate people—instead, he will allow justice to blossom.

The road of taking up the cross and denying oneself means being free from those values that would crush the spirits of others. So Jesus is teaching us to be servants—and to be a servant Church. What are your aims? What are your spiritual aims? Are they to be 'more powerful' in terms of abilities and gifts, or to be more humble? Maybe this passage gives us the clue to real spirituality.

There's a hint of something else in verse 8 when Jesus says, 'Unless I wash you, you have no share with me.' Unless we let Jesus serve us, we can't be his disciples. Maybe there's a hint of the waters of baptism here, of letting Jesus baptize us. But Jesus baptizes just the feet. Is this an echo of Isaiah 52:7, 'How beautiful upon the mountains are the feet of the messenger who announces peace, who brings good news, who announces salvation.' The disciples are being baptized for the task to go out and serve, to bring the good news to the poor, to proclaim peace and salvation. And to obey means walking in the right direction, being a servant and, for that, having baptized feet!

Then Jesus sits down and he makes sure the disciples understand this acted parable. He uses the word 'Lord' of himself. This is the one time that he talks this way. He says, 'If I, your Lord and Teacher, have washed your feet, you also ought to wash one another's feet.' A lord normally exerts dominion over others, whereas a servant gives himself. Jesus is revealing the nature of God. He is the Lord who serves. This is the hope for a proud, warring, wilful world: the way of the servant, being set free to serve one another and to build a community of peace; to walk away from the old ways of domination and greed and the wrong use of power.

To think about

Put yourself in Peter's place. Imagine Jesus kneeling in front of you. Does it seem right? Would your response differ from Peter? Then allow Jesus to wash your feet, to serve you. And then sit and listen to his explanation.

Maundy Thursday
The bread and the wine

LUKE 22:19–22

Then he took a loaf of bread, and when he had given thanks, he broke it and gave it to them, saying, 'This is my body, which is given for you. Do this in remembrance of me.' And he did the same with the cup after supper, saying, 'This cup that is poured out for you is the new covenant in my blood. But, see, the one who betrays me is with me, and his hand is on the table. For the Son of Man is going as it has been determined, but woe to that one by whom he is betrayed!'

Yesterday we thought about baptized feet and the disciples going out to bring good news and to proclaim peace. But a pair of those feet were not clean, as Jesus had pointed out at the time. One pair of feet were heading in the wrong direction—Judas didn't want Jesus to serve, he wanted him to dominate. And he goes out from the light of the world and into the darkness. John makes this very clear as he talks about Judas receiving the bread and then he says, 'he immediately went out' adding the cryptic comment—'it was night'. If we are prepared to be followers of Jesus this is the food for our journey, this is the food to give us the strength for the task ahead. Jesus enacting the drama that will also help us remember what he has done *for* us and that he is *with* us.

It's the meal that unites, it's the meal of communion or fellowship. One of my privileges, because I travel a lot, is that I have had communion in churches all around the world of totally varying styles, from very grand cathedrals to little churches with tin roofs, and right across all denominational divides. I remember vividly one night in Norway walking to a eucharist at midnight. It was in summertime, so it was not properly dark even at midnight, which gave me a strange feeling. The service was a Nicaraguan mass, it was led by a Lutheran priest, the music group was from Bolivia and the preacher was a Methodist from the Dominican Republic! It seemed so symbolic of unity—with people of different denominations, and from different parts of the world, united together, acting out this drama that Jesus had told us to do.

I've had the opportunity to be at the most awe-inspiring and mystical of communion services or masses and at the most simple, and it always seems to me they are moments of refreshment, moments of encounter with God himself. It is here that Jesus serves us and feeds us. He serves us so we can serve others. Sadly, at the Reformation, the meal that unites became the meal that divides, but Jesus' last prayer for his followers in John 17 was that we should 'be one' and we must seek to restore that uniting factor in this meal. After all, its significance is forgiveness and reconciliation.

The taking of the bread and wine signifies feeding on Jesus. 'I am the Bread of Life.' He is our staple diet. When Jesus, in John 6, after the feeding of the 5,000, talks about the need for us to feed on him, he says powerful and shocking words, and yet words of great encouragement. We need Jesus for life in all its fulness. Just as we could not have had life in the first place without the breath of the creator, so we cannot grow in the new life without the spiritual food of Jesus. John 15 also reminds us that, 'I am the true vine, and you are the branches.' We are to remain in Jesus—our relationship must be that close. He is the wine of the new covenant, as the miracle of the turning water into wine showed. And to take the bread and the wine is a moment of encounter and commitment. We 'take and eat', to change us, to equip us for the work.

In the eucharist Jesus meets every need. In a special way, he meets us. This is the point of forgiveness, of healing, of comfort. It's the place where minds are changed, where prejudices are recognized and removed, and the key act is a reminder of God inside us, by his Spirit. We remember his death, so we can live, forgiven. This is the place to ask God to search our motives, the place of starting afresh, of drawing strength for the task, it is the place of relief, of joy. And so we share, by this act, in his death and resurrection. 'May we who share Christ's body live his risen life.' So, this Easter, take time to feed on the bread and the wine of the new kingdom. Receive this gift of Jesus to equip you as a servant and to follow the compassionate king and his upside-down kingdom.

Prayer

Lord Christ, you remain, unseen, at our side, present like a poor man who washes the feet of his friends. And we, to follow in your footsteps, we are here, waiting for you to suggest signs of sharing to make us into the servants of your gospel. Amen.

Brother Roger of Taizé

Good Friday
The vulnerable God

LUKE 22:42, 52–53

'Father if you are willing, remove this cup from me; yet, not my will but yours be done.'… Then Jesus said to the chief priests, the officers of the temple police, and the elders who had come for him, 'Have you come out with swords and clubs as if I were a bandit? When I was with you day after day in the temple, you did not lay hands on me. But this is your hour, and the power of darkness!'

So after the Passover meal, he went on to the Mount of Olives and Luke says, 'as was his custom'. It was his place to be quiet, his place to pray. He prays that, if it is God's will, the cup of suffering will be removed yet, nevertheless, he is ready to accept God's will. The Garden of Gethsemane, on the Mount of Olives, is a beautiful place. It's the other side of the Kidron Valley, outside the city. Today there is a church built over the spot where they say Jesus may have prayed. This church, the Church of All Nations, is a particularly striking one. Outside there are eight very ancient olive trees, which they say are from Roman times. They give a reminder of where Jesus would have knelt and prayed, surrounded by olive trees. The church itself is particularly beautiful. There is subdued violet blue light coming through the windows which are made of alabaster. It gives it a most beautiful atmosphere and there is a sense of quiet and prayer. It is a place to stay and focus one's thoughts.

The cross is our example and our route. It is the heart of our faith. And it is the route Jesus now takes. I remember once, when I was in Malaysia, meeting with Archbishop Anthony Soter Fernandez. He is the Catholic Archbishop of Malaysia. When he was installed he chose two quotations, one by Dietrich Bonhoeffer, 'When the Lord calls, he bids us come and die' and the second from Galatians 1:10, 'If I were still pleasing people, I would not be a servant of Christ.' He is a man of tremendous courage and deep understanding of the implications of the gospel. The security police came to his home, on one occasion, in the middle of the night and when they came in, it was almost like an echo of Jesus talking to the temple police. He said to the security men, 'Only robbers call at night' and so he insisted they sign the guest book so that he could treat them as guests. It is quite amusing to look at his guest book and see the string of names. He knows that following the way of Christ needs to be a way of courage and, indeed, a journey that could lead to crucifixion.

Brother Ramon, in his book, *The Way of Love* says, 'Good Friday—a bad day if ever there was one. This was the day on which the incarnation of the divine love was taken, unjustly condemned, beaten and cruelly crucified by the hands of his creatures. And yet it was a day so good that it manifested the length and the depths to which love would go to reconcile the world to himself.' So the way of the cross is the way of love, and from the cross there streams love, reconciliation, forgiveness… and hope.

To think about

Last Easter, the Christians from the West Bank were not allowed to come into Jerusalem to walk the way of the cross even though, geographically, they are so close. The curfew on the West Bank meant they could not join the Christians who had come from all over the world to remember the death and the resurrection of Jesus. Pray that, out of their struggle and pain, a resurrection hope will rise.

Prayer

Lord: Help us to see in the groaning of creation not death throes but birth pangs; help us to see in suffering a promise for the future, because it is a cry against the inhumanity of the present. Help us to glimpse in protest the dawn of justice, in the cross the pathway to resurrection, and in suffering the seeds of joy.

Rubem Alves, Brazil, from *All Year Round*, British Council of Churches, 1987

For meditation

Jesus of the Scars

If we have never sought, we seek you now;
Your eyes burn through the dark our only stars;
We must have sight of thorn marks on your brow
We must have you O Jesus of the scars.

The heavens frighten us, they are too calm;
In all the universe we have no place.
Our wounds are hurting us, where is the balm?
Lord Jesus by your scars we know your grace.

O Jesus of the scars we seek you now
O Jesus of the scars we seek you now;
We must have sight of thorn marks on your brow
We must have you O Jesus of the scars.

The other gods were strong, but you were weak;
They rode, but you did stumble to a throne;
But to our wounds only God's wounds can speak,
And not a god has wounds, but you alone.

O Jesus of the scars we seek you now
O Jesus of the scars we seek you now;
We must have sight of thorn marks on your brow
We must have you O Jesus of the scars.

Edward Shillito,
adapted by Garth Hewitt

Easter Eve
A day of waiting

LUKE 23:44–46; 50–53

It was now about noon, and darkness came over the whole land until three in the afternoon, while the sun's light failed; and the curtain of the temple was torn in two. Then Jesus, crying with a loud voice, said, 'Father into your hands I commend my spirit.' Having said this, he breathed his last... Now there was a good and righteous man named Joseph... He came from the Jewish town of Arimathea, and he was waiting expectantly for the kingdom of God. This man went to Pilate and asked for the body of Jesus. Then he took it down, wrapped it in a linen cloth, and laid it in a rock-hewn tomb where no one had ever been laid.

So Jesus dies. And although we, with the benefit of hindsight, know what is coming tomorrow, for the early disciples it was not like that. We have seen, in Luke's Gospel, Jesus repeatedly mention his death and resurrection but, in each case, without the disciples understanding. I think we all can empathize with this. Put yourself in the position of the disciples. It would be a hard thing to understand. The sense of loss and the sense of failure and the sense that everything had ended must have been great, as Jesus died on the cross. Yet there was something about this death that clearly moved the centurion, and in Luke he declares Jesus innocent, whereas Mark has him saying that 'Truly this was the Son of God.'

For the disciples it must have been a time of sadness, a sense of bereavement, a time of thinking, trying to recollect different things that he had said. Peter had said, 'You are the Christ, you are the anointed one.' The gospel has shown us he truly is the anointed one, but anointed for what? Anointed for his death. In the Eastern Church, icons show Christ attacking the gates of hell and death. This is, so to speak, his activity on this day before bursting into glory on Easter morning. There is a very pregnant pause.

It's a time of leaving people with their thoughts. Obviously Mary, the mother of Jesus, must have experienced the pain of it all in a very special way. Certainly that prophecy of Simeon had come true, that a sword would pierce her own soul. We know that Mary was someone who treasured things and pondered them, and she must have felt the pain of this day very deeply. How did Mary and Martha feel, Mary Magdalen and Lazarus? Peter was perhaps grappling with his own denial earlier in the week. Peter had said that Jesus is the Christ, and was then soon told off by Jesus for trying to discourage him from taking the journey to Jerusalem: Peter, who learns by making mistakes; Peter, who will be fishing up in Galilee in a few days' time and will meet Jesus again in one of his resurrection appearances, and will be asked three times, 'Do you love me?' and will be hurt when he is asked the third time, 'Do you love me?' And he will respond, 'Lord, you know everything, you know that I love you.' Then he will be told again to 'feed my sheep' and warned of his own death, and then told, 'Follow me.'

What a devastating moment for Peter: Peter, who loves deeply, who gets it wrong with enthusiasm, and who learns from mistakes. What a remarkable moment. And Peter then gets it wrong again and asks, 'What about him?' pointing to the disciple Jesus loved. And Jesus says, 'What is that to you? Follow me.'

I like people who learn by mistakes, because those who don't make mistakes rarely learn as deeply. Peter's problem may have been his enthusiasm, his impetuousness, and he rushes in wrong directions. But his love is deep and genuine, and the story is told that when he came to die, and they were crucifying him, he asked to be crucified upside-down because he was not worthy to die in the same way as his Lord had died—I can believe that, it sounds typical of Peter. But today he is probably wrestling with all sorts of emotions, and the memory of having denied the one he had walked with for three years.

You may take some time today to think of mistakes, failures, times you have let people down. Face up to them and learn from them. Peter did, and he took the Church of Christ forward in an extraordinary way. Ask God to let you be someone who learns from mistakes.

Prayer

I rest, with you Jesus, in the tomb.
I wait, with you Jesus, for the new creation.

Margaret Hebbelthwaite, *Through Lent with Luke*, BRF

Prayer

O holy wisdom of our God,
Eternally offensive to our wisdom,
And compassionate towards our weakness,
We praise you and give you thanks,

Because you emptied yourself of power
And entered our struggle,
Taking upon you unprotected flesh.
You opened wide your arms for us upon the cross,
Becoming scandal for our sake,
That you might sanctify even the grave
To be a bed of hope to your people.

We praise you, saying:
Holy, holy, holy,
Vulnerable God.
Heaven and earth are full of your glory;
Hosanna in the highest.
Blessed is the one
Who comes in the name of God;
Hosanna in the highest.

Janet Morley, Christian Aid

Easter Sunday
The road to Emmaus

Luke 24:13–35

Now on that same day two of them were going to a village called Emmaus, about seven miles from Jerusalem, and talking with each other about all these things that had happened. While they were talking and discussing, Jesus himself came near and went with them, but their eyes were kept from recognizing him...

As they came near the village to which they were going, he walked ahead as if he were going on. But they urged him strongly, saying, 'Stay with us, because it is almost evening and the day is now nearly over.' So he went in to stay with them. When he was at table with them, he took bread, blessed and broke it, and gave it to them. Then their eyes were opened, and they recognized him; and he vanished from their sight... That same hour they got up and returned to Jerusalem... Then they told what had happened on the road, and how he had been made known to them in the breaking of the bread.

One of Luke's themes has been that of 'journeying' and for him it's an image of discipleship, and he's also used the theme of 'seeing'. We notice that the disciples couldn't 'see', in the sense of 'understand', when they were heading up to Jerusalem, and now, their eyes are kept from recognizing him. Although they have heard of the resurrection from the women at the tomb, they still have not got the eyes of faith. But these disciples, who are prepared to entertain a stranger, are about to have their eyes opened and as Jesus does his most familiar sign, by taking bread, blessing it, breaking it, and giving it to them, this act opens their eyes. So the eyes of faith are opened, joy replaces the sorrow and the bewilderment, God's kingdom is here, and there is a task to be done.

And when we are on the journey, and feel lost or bewildered, let us remember to show hospitality, do acts of kindness, for in the very doing of them our eyes may be opened. And, also, let us partake in the breaking of bread, for this is where Christ meets us and makes himself known to us, in our hospitality to strangers and in our fellowship at the eucharist.

And what of our present day Christians and peacemakers whom we have met in the Holy Land? What does Emmaus say to them? In some ways, it is a painful moment because, though it is not clear exactly which is the site of Emmaus (there are four possible ones) the oldest is Amwas or Emmaus. Here there are the ruins of the Emmaus basilica and also a crusader church. And here you will find Canada Park, a wooden recreation centre, created by the Israelis over the ruins of three Palestinian villages, Yalu, Beit Nuba and Amwas or Emmaus. The villages were destroyed in 1967 and their inhabitants expelled. The well-known Israeli reporter, Amos Kenan, wrote a report of the razing of these villages. He describes how the villages were beautiful and the houses and the trees, but 'with one sweep of the bulldozer, the cypresses and the olive trees were uprooted. Ten or more minutes pass and the house, with its meagre furnishings and belongings, had become a mass of rubble… The fields were turned to desolation before our eyes and the children who dragged themselves along the road that day, weeping bitterly, will be the *fedayeen* of nineteen years hence. This is how that day we lost the victory' (Amos Kenan, *Israel: A Victory Wasted*).

That is one of the suggested sites of Emmaus. Another is Qalunieh. This, too, was a Palestinian village that was destroyed, in 1948, situated just off the modern highway to Tel Aviv. There is nothing to view at this site but it does seem to be about the right geographical distance for the disciples to have returned to Jerusalem that night. So, if we are tempted to make this a rather romantic passage of Jesus walking with the disciples along the Emmaus road, we are brought up sharply as we think of Emmaus in the current situation, for two of the suggested sites are scenes of pain and suffering.

Our passage reminds us of hospitality. Hospitality must be shown to the refugee, the alien, the stranger. And the history of the Jewish people has been to be aliens and strangers who have suffered, so often at the hands of Christians, through the centuries. The history of present-day Palestinians is to be aliens and strangers in their own land. If we have learnt anything as we have walked with Jesus through the Holy Land, it must be that he espoused the ways of non-violence, that he rejected domination, that he came to serve all people and to show us how to love our neighbour, and to give us the strength to do this, and to meet us in the breaking of bread.

Pray not for Arab or Jew
For Palestinian or Israeli
But pray rather for ourselves
That we might not divide them in our prayers
But keep them both together in our hearts.

Christian Aid; based on a prayer by a Palestinian Christian

*For there is a question that haunts the festival of Pesach (Passover).
Why did God bring it about that the Jewish people should be born in
exile, forged in slavery, and made to suffer brutal oppression? To this
the Bible gives an unequivocal answer. You shall not do what others
have done to you. 'Do not oppress the stranger because you know
what it feels like to be a stranger: You were strangers in the land of
Egypt.' What you suffered you shall not inflict. You experienced
injustice, therefore practise justice. You know what it is like to be a
slave, therefore do not enslave others. You have been victims,
therefore you may not be oppressors. You have been murdered,
therefore do not join the ranks of the murderers. Until we understand
this we have not understood Judaism, however religious we are.*

Rabbi Jonathan Sacks, Chief Rabbi of the United
Hebrew Congregations of the Commonwealth,
(from *Faith in the Future*, published by DLT)

Forward to our Galilee

And for us, we started our journey in Jerusalem and heading down the Jericho road, we have headed up the Jordan valley, after taking our detour into the Bethlehem area, and then we went on into Galilee, right up to the border with Syria at Caesarea Philippi, and then we journeyed down via Jericho, up to Bethany, across the Kidron, into Jerusalem. Now, maybe we've taken our journey with Jesus down the road some way towards Tel Aviv. And, as twentieth-century pilgrims, no doubt we will fly home from Tel Aviv. But what are the disciples told? They are told that Jesus has gone ahead of them into Galilee. It's almost as if it goes full circle. There is work to be done, to carry on the work of Jesus.

And wherever we are, it is our Galilee, where we are called to be disciples, where we are called to keep walking, where we will always find that Christ has gone before us, a peacemaker in a world that has no peace, a healer in a world that is broken, a saviour in a world that needs to be saved from its selfishness, its pride, its violence and its greed. Before we lose sight of Jesus, let's find him again in the poor and the forgotten, let's find him in the breaking of the bread, let's draw our strength, let's find our forgiveness, let's walk towards wholeness, the wholeness of life that he offers. And though we may walk through valleys of despair, and through times of crucifixion, we are never without this resurrection hope because we are the community of hope, the community of love, the community of Jesus.

In Him We Saw A Man Fully Living

In him we knew a fulness never known before,
In him we saw a man fully living.

In him we see the God who can't be seen;
In him all things that will be, or have been,
Have roots and take their being.

In him we knew a fulness never known before,
In him we saw a man fully living.

The universe and all its millions teeming,
Seen and unseen, in him find their meaning,
Their reason and their value.

In him we knew a fulness never known before,
In him we saw a man fully living.

He lives in those who, breathing with his breath,
Source of their life, and conquerer of their death,
Together form his body.

In him we knew a fulness never known before,
In him we saw a man fully living.

Through him alone a world by sin defiled
Finds its forgiveness, and is reconciled,
His death our peace and healing.

In him we knew a fulness never known before,
In him we saw a man fully living.

From St Paul to the Colossians 1:15–20,
translated by H.J. Richards, copyright
1994 Kevin Mayhew Ltd.

Liturgies

I use these two liturgies on visits to the Holy Land—I have adapted them from the *Wee Worship Book* of the Iona Community. Groups may like to use the Nazareth liturgy in Nazareth and Galilee and the Jerusalem liturgy in Jerusalem and the surrounding areas.

Jerusalem Liturgy

Leader: Come Lord Jesus
You too were tired
When day was done;
You met your friends at evening time.
All: *COME, LORD JESUS.*
Leader: You too came to Jerusalem
But you came with determination,
With tasks to be done.
All: *COME, LORD JESUS.*
Leader: You came to show us the way
Of a humble king—a serving Lord
To be the crucified one
And to show us how to live.
All: *COME, LORD JESUS.*
Leader: Come, Lord Jesus,
You too enjoyed when nights drew on
To tell your tales at close of day.
All: *COME, LORD JESUS.*
Leader: Come, Lord Jesus,
You kindled faith when lamps were low;
You opened scriptures, broke the bread
And shed your light as darkness fell.
All: *COME, LORD JESUS, MEET US HERE.*

Song

Prayer

Leader: Let us pray.
You broke down the barriers
When you crept in beside us.
For in Jesus... the smiling Jesus,

... the storytelling Jesus,
... the controversial Jesus,
... the annoying Jesus,
... the loving and forgiving Jesus,
Yours hands touched all, and touched us
Showing how in Christ there is neither Jew nor Gentile
neither male nor female:
All: *ALL ARE ONE IN JESUS CHRIST, AND FOR THIS WE PRAISE YOU.*
Leader: You opened our eyes
To see how the hands of the rich were empty
And the hearts of the poor were full.
You dared to take the widow's mite,
the child's loaves,
the babe at the breast,
And in these simple things
To point out the path to your Kingdom.
You said, 'Follow me',
For on our own we could never discover
That in Christ there is neither Jew nor Gentile,
neither male nor female:
All: *ALL ARE ONE IN JESUS CHRIST, AND FOR THIS WE PRAISE YOU.*
Leader: You gave us hands to hold:
Black hands and white hands,
African hands and Asian hands,
The clasping hands of lovers,
And the reluctant hands of those
Who don't believe they are worth holding.
And when we wanted to shake our fist,
You still wanted to hold our hand,
Because in Christ there is neither Jew nor Gentile,
Neither male nor female:
All: *ALL ARE ONE IN JESUS CHRIST, AND FOR THIS WE PRAISE YOU.*
AMEN.

Reading

Blessing

Leader: May God bless us
In our sleep with rest
In our dreams with vision
In our waking with a calm mind
In our souls with the friendship of the Holy Spirit
This night and every night.
All: *AMEN.*

Nazareth Liturgy

Leader: Lord, here we are in Nazareth—the town of your formative years
Here we are so close to the sight of the synagogue
Where you stood up and proclaimed:
'The Spirit of the Lord is upon me
Because he has anointed me to bring good news to the poor
He has sent me to proclaim release to the captives
Recovery of sight to the blind
To let the oppressed go free
To proclaim the year of the Lord's favour.'
And as every eye was on you in the synagogue
You said, 'Today this scripture has been fulfilled in your hearing.'
And the wonderful words of this Nazareth mandate
Go down through the centuries and remind us
of the tasks of the Kingdom of God
And the hope of the Kingdom of God.
And as we say our liturgy tonight, we ask that we
will be people of the Kingdom,
We will be people of your way,
We will be the people of the Good News to all who are poor or oppressed.
So let the day end, the night fall, the world move into silence,
And let God's people say Amen.
All: *AMEN*
Leader: Let minds unwind, hearts be still, bodies relax,
And let God's people say Amen.
All: *AMEN*
Leader: But before the day is done
Let God's holy name be praised
And let God's people say Amen.
All: *AMEN*

Song

Prayer

Leader: Christ is the source of all life.
All: *HE BRINGS LIGHT TO THE WORLD.*
Leader: The light shines in the darkness,
All: *AND THE DARKNESS CAN NEVER PUT IT OUT.*
Leader: He came to his own,
All: *AND HIS OWN DID NOT RECEIVE HIM.*
Leader: Yet to those who believe in him,
He gives the right to become God's children.

Let us pray:
Creator, Son and Spirit
One God in perfect community
Look now on us who look to you
And hear our prayer this night.

Where there is any falseness
All: *SMOTHER IT BY YOUR TRUTH.*
Leader: Where there is coldness
All: *KINDLE THE FLAME WITH YOUR LOVE.*
Leader: Where there is any resentment
All: *SHOW US THE ROAD TO COMPASSION.*
Leader: Where there is anything we will not do for ourselves
All: *MAKE US DISCONTENT UNTIL IT IS DONE.*
Leader: And make us one,
All: *AS YOU ARE ONE.*
Leader: From Nazareth you came down to Jerusalem
To the way of the cross.
Let us pray that we may see the way to the cross
And the way beyond it.
Help us, Lord, to follow where you walk,
To stop where you stumble,
To grieve where you die,
To dance where you rise again,
Knowing that this is the only way
There is no other way.
All: *AMEN.*

Reading

Blessing

Leader: May God bless you,
May he keep you ever in his care
And lead your lives with love.
All: *MAY GOD'S WARM WELCOME SHINE FROM OUR HEARTS, AND CHRIST'S OWN PEACE PREVAIL THROUGH EVERY DAY TILL GREATER LIFE SHALL CALL. AMEN.*

Group study material

Here is material for discussion groups for each week of our journey in *Pilgrims and Peacemakers*.

Each week

Each week I would suggest you look at the relevant map in the weekly introduction and also at the map in the front of the book to see the wider context. If anyone has visited the area that is the focus for the week they could share their thoughts and experiences. Each week in the book there are a variety of Bible passages that could be studied and also some stories of people who are local Christians and peacemakers—I've sometimes suggested ones you could use but feel free to use the other material or the prayers and to vary it to suit your group.

It would be good if the group are able to read the appropriate week in advance of the discussion and then talk about those things which stand out—those that are a help or other things that even worry people or with which they want to disagree— take time each week to draw out some of these points.

Week one: The wilderness

After looking at the map, talk about deserts and wilderness—do they attract you— do they make you fearful?

You might like to discuss wilderness experiences—maybe you feel you're in one— have you been through one?

Read Luke 4:1–14 then look at Ash Wednesday's notes and read the first paragraph and discuss the temptations of the 'easy road'.

Look at the 'thought' at the end of the day and also at Archbishop Tutu's comments as part of your discussion.

What are our 'idols'? Thursday's notes give us some clues.

What are the 'Spiritual' temptations?

Discuss the parable of 'The Good Samaritan' and it's implications for us.

Look at the 'thought' at the end of Saturday's notes and discuss what this means.

Finally pray about the lessons learnt from what you've discussed both about temptation and about how we should imitate the Good Samaritan.

Then look at Gaza on the map and pray for the churches there and read Winnie Tarizi's comment or Rabbi Jeremy Milgrom's in 'Journeying to Peace'—pray for this crowded piece of land of Gaza and for the church and the peacemakers there.

Week two: Bethlehem

Read Bishara Awad's comments under 'Message of love from Bethlehem'—in the week's introductory comments—especially paragraph two and read one or two of the Bible readings for the week.

Then look at Kenneth Leech's quote at the end of Monday's notes concerning Bethlehem and Calvary and discuss the significance of the style of Jesus' birth at Bethlehem.

Do we sometimes lose track of this in the 'romanticism' of Christmas time?

Read the story of Beit Jala's rehabilitation centre on Friday and then discuss the 'thought' at the end—does your church have any refugees—do you support work with refugees—are there some practical steps to be taken?

Then discuss 'Jesus the vulnerable child' and the last paragraph of Saturday's notes concerning street kids—how should we respond?

How do we say 'no' to the ways of Herod and 'yes' to the ways of Jesus?

Pray for the homeless, refugees, street children—pray through lessons learnt from the birth of Jesus.

Pray for the Christians of the Bethlehem area—Bishara Awad at Bethlehem Bible College and Salim Manayer who is also there—pray for his reconciliation work 'Musalaha' and Josef Shulam of the Messianic Jewish Community. Pray for the Christians of Beit Sahour who have suffered so much and for Beit Jala's wonderful work of healing.

Week three: Nazareth and Capernaum

Read Luke 4:6–21 and read the first paragraph of Wednesday's notes.

Read some of Riah's comments on Thursday—don't leave out his last sentence 'I confess one of my weaknesses... is optimism.'

Look at Saturday's notes—'Jesus moves to Capernaum' and read the paragraph 'Have we lost the excitement of this new kingdom...'

Talk about how the gospel should work in Britain (or your country) and discuss how we can bring down mountains and valleys can be lifted up. What does this mean in practice?

Discuss peace—look at Audeh Rantisi's story on Sunday—his flight as a refugee— his discovery of peace with God and then look at Zahi Nasser's words about the quality of life God has intended for us in 'Journeying to peace'. How can we be peacemakers?

Take time to pray through lessons learnt—pray for the Christian community in Nazareth, especially Christ Church and Bishop Riah Abu El-Assal and pray for the Christians in Lydda and Zahi Nasser and in Ramallah with Audeh Rantisi.

Finish by praying Janet Morley's prayer (Wednesday).

Week four: Galilee

Read Matthew 5:1–9 (or more if you'd like to). Then close your eyes and visualize sitting by the sea of Galilee on the Mount of Beatitudes and get someone to read

Abuna Elias Chacour's words on 'the mounts of closeness' (Thursday)—from the first paragraph through to 'you are in the lowest place in the world'.

Then discuss the two mountains and what Jesus is saying to us on 'the mountains of closeness'.

It would be good if the group could read in advance the parable of 'The three trees and an open house' (fourth Sunday) and also Yehezkal Landau's thoughts 'Journeying to peace' called 'Peace movements and biblical faith'—then discuss this venture in practical peacemaking and lessons to be learnt from it.

Pray for Elias Chacour and his school in Ibillin in Galilee, for Mubarak Awad and the Palestinian Centre for Non-violence in Jerusalem and for Yehezkal and Dalia Landau and Michail Fanous at 'Open House' at Ramle.

Also pray through lessons learnt from 'The sermon on the mount'—thank God for the 'mountain of closeness' and the implications of this message.

Week five: Northern Galilee

Read Matthew 6:7–15

This could be followed by a time of quiet to think through some of the phrases of the Lord's Prayer.

Then discuss it—talk about what the various parts mean to you.

Look at the 'thought' on Tuesday and talk about Jesus and who people think he is and how we can better communicate him to our own society (maybe refer to Matthew 16:13–20).

Discuss the lessons of the father and son reunion (Saturday) the father running to bring reconciliation—maybe people could try and put themselves in the position of the two sons or the father or even the local community—what would you think?—where would you be surprised? Different people could take different roles.

Then have a time of quiet to work through how you would respond and then share your thoughts.

On Sunday Elijah encounters a sense of God in the 'sheer silence'—have some time of silence to think through lessons learnt in Northern Galilee and also to simply 'be still' before God.

Pray through your lessons learnt, pray for two women peacemakers—Lynda Brayer—a Christian lawyer and Roni Ben Efrat—the courageous activist and also pray for the Reverend Shehadeh Shehadeh and his church of St John's in Haifa and the other Christian communities who are living and worshipping there.

Week six: Towards Jerusalem

This is the week of changed lives—use the prayer 'Forgive us our divisions' at the introduction to the week—and then read the passage in John 4:5–14 about the woman of the well.

Why was the woman so surprised that Jesus spoke to her?

Discuss Jesus' attitude to women.

Read Cedar Duaybis' story (Tuesday) and discuss how Jesus makes people whole.

Zaccheus was changed by his meeting with, and acceptance by, Jesus—look at Thursday's thought and take time to think about things that you think need changing.

Jerusalem—look at Friday, the passages and the first paragraph—Jesus comes as the way of peace for this city of pain—what are the clues he gave that show us the way for peace in that troubled city?

Use Gerald Butts lovely prayer—have a time of prayer and pray for justice and peace for the Holy Land.

In a further time of quiet and meditation imagine that you are Jesus pausing at Bethany before all that is to come—then one person read 'Tomorrow the Kidron Valley' (Saturday).

Week seven: Jerusalem

Pray the 'prayer for Jerusalem' by Najwa Farah—choose one of the readings of this week—perhaps the one from the day on which you are discussing this.

What tables of exploitation or wrong attitudes need turning over in our society?

Discuss how you would feel about Jesus serving you as in the incident of the feet washing—would you react like Peter?

Gethsemane—let someone read the passage in Luke about the garden of Gethsemane—then have a time of quiet to think through Jesus' own attitude at this time—finish the silence by reading the Eucharistic prayer 'O Holy wisdom of our God' (Saturday).

'Jesus of the Scars' could be read as an additional meditation.

Take time to pray for the pilgrims and peacemakers we've met on our journey—the Christians and peacemakers of Jerusalem like Bishop Samir Kafity, Canon Naim Ateek, Lynda Brayer, the many others—any known to you.

Pray for the many churches of Jerusalem—for unity amongst them—for their witness to Christ and to his way of peace.

Use the Christian Aid prayer at the end of Easter Sunday 'Pray not for Arab or Jew...'